Developing and Managing Electronic Collections

DEVELOPING AND
MANAGING
ELECTRONIC COLLECTIONS

THE ESSENTIALS

PEGGY JOHNSON

An imprint of the American Library Association // Chicago // 2013

PEGGY JOHNSON is a frequent speaker and trainer on collection development and management. She has published several books, including ALA Editions' bestselling *Fundamentals of Collection Development and Management,* and numerous journal articles. She edited the peer-reviewed journal *Library Resources and Technical Services* for more than nine years, ending her term in December 2012, and continues to edit *Technicalities: Information Forum for the Technical Services Professional.* Prior to retiring from the University of Minnesota Libraries, she served as associate university librarian. Peggy is past president of the Association for Library Collections and Technical Services and received the ALCTS Ross Atkinson Lifetime Achievement Award in 2009. She has a Masters from the University of Chicago Graduate Library School and a Master's of Management and Administration from Metropolitan State University.

Printed in the United States of America

17 16 15 14 13   5 4 3 2 1

Extensive effort has gone into ensuring the reliability of the information in this book; however, the publisher makes no warranty, express or implied, with respect to the material contained herein.

ISBNs: 978-0-8389-1190-7 (paper); 978–0-8389-9615-7 (PDF); 978-8389-9616-4 (ePub); 978-8389-9617-1 (Kindle). For more information on digital formats, visit the ALA Store at alastore.ala.org and select eEditions.

Library of Congress Cataloging-in-Publication Data

Johnson, Peggy, 1948-
    Developing and managing electronic collections : the essentials /
Peggy Johnson.
        pages   cm
    Includes bibliographical references and index.
    ISBN 978-0-8389-1190-7 (alk. paper)
1. Libraries—Special collections—Electronic information resources.
2. Electronic information resources—Management. 3. Libraries and
electronic publishing—United States. I. Title.
    Z692.C65J64 2013
    025.2'84—dc23   2013005038

Cover design by Kimberly Thornton. Cover image © Shutterstock, Inc.
Text design by Adrianna Sutton in Minion Pro and Gotham.

⊗ This paper meets the requirements of ANSI/NISO Z39.48-1992 (Permanence of Paper).

CONTENTS

PREFACE

The logical place to begin a book that explores electronic collections is with a shared understanding of what *electronic collections* means. Many terms—*virtual library, electronic* or *e-library, digital library,* and more—are used interchangeably to refer to a library that collects digital resources. For the purposes of this book, electronic collections are the electronic content selected by librarians from a variety of sources for a library, managed by the library, and made available for users. This content may be purchased, leased, or available as free resources. It may be selected title by title or in bundled packages. The emphasis in this book is on developing and managing this type of collection, particularly content accessed via the Internet.

As library collections in all types of libraries increasingly become electronic, librarians are faced with both opportunities and challenges. These include coping with rising costs while meeting increasing user expectations, understanding copyright and fair use in the digital environment, following rapidly changing technologies, negotiating licenses and contracts, and tracking evolving business models. During the process of writing this book, I researched and monitored developments in these areas and consulted with librarians about their practices. I have done my best to incorporate current information while providing practical information that will guide librarians in their work with electronic content, a challenge during such a volatile time.

This book is scoped to be generally applicable to all types of libraries. All books, by their finite nature, are limited in various ways. I have intentionally omitted some digital formats and genres (e.g., textbooks, games, software, locally produced datasets, locally digitized content). Some topics, such as open access, I introduce but do not explore in depth. Resources and tools for locating e-content are not included. Although promoting e-collections and assisting patrons in their use are important responsibilities for libraries, they are not addressed in this book. Information about publishers, vendors, agents, aggregators, and other suppliers was accurate at the time of this writing, but the marketplace is changing rapidly and readers should carefully research options before making decisions. I intend references to individual companies to be exemplars that do not imply endorsement.

Selecting e-content for libraries is the responsibility of various people, who have different titles and differing assignments in their libraries. For convenience, I use *selector* as the descriptive title for those who select resources to add (either through purchase or subscription) to the collection.

A persistent theme in this book is the multifaceted, nonlinear, and often cross-departmental nature of developing and managing e-collections. Separating interconnected and interdependent topics and associated tasks into logical chapter divisions creates somewhat artificial divisions. Negotiating contracts and licenses is not possible without understanding their nature and components. Selecting e-content effectively depends on understanding selection and acquisition options in the e-content market. So, although each chapter covers a specific topic, it is best understood within the context of the book as a whole.

Each chapter, except chapter 9, is followed by a list of suggested readings. Sources in these lists and those cited in each chapter are drawn from contemporary professional literature, news, and websites. Each URL was accurate at the time this book was completed. A glossary offers definitions of terms.

My goal is to offer practical guidance in navigating the complex issues associated with developing and managing electronic collections in libraries of all types and sizes. To that end, chapters explore key issues and decision points and offer advice on best practices for developing and managing these important resources. This book aims to provide an understanding of the context in which electronic collection development and management occur and to offer practical solutions that provide effective, efficient, and timely access to online resources for library users.

ACKNOWLEDGMENTS

Books are not written in isolation, and this one is no exception. Friends and colleagues graciously shared their advice, information, and expertise as I researched and wrote this book. I thank especially Steven Bosch (University of Arizona Libraries), Eric Celeste (independent library technology consultant), Ginny Brodeen (Contemporary Library Consultants), Nadine Ellero (Auburn University), Fariha Grieme (University of Minnesota Libraries), Gary Handman (Moffitt Library, University of California Berkeley), Cindy Hepfer and Susan Davis (University at Buffalo Libraries), Brian Karschnia and John Larson (St. Paul Public Library), David Lesniaski and Heidi Hammond (St. Catherine University Master of Library and Information Science program), Bob Nardini (Coutts), Narda Tafuri (University of Scranton Library), and Michael Zeoli and Hester Campbell (YBP Library Services). ˙

Researching is much different than when I began my writing career, with many resources available online, but interlibrary loan remains an essential library service. My thanks for speedy delivery of the innumerable books and articles I have consulted go to the ILL staff at the University of Minnesota Libraries: Cherie Weston, Melissa Eighmy Brown, Guy Peterson, Emily Riha, and Alice Welch. My dear friend Bonnie MacEwan (Auburn University), who graciously read each chapter, contributed to the clarity and completeness of this book. All errors and omissions are solely my responsibility. I cannot conclude without thanking my eternally patient and supportive husband, Lee, to whom this book is dedicated.

CHAPTER 1

OVERVIEW OF THE EVOLVING ELECTRONIC COLLECTIONS ENVIRONMENT

MANAGING AND DEVELOPING electronic collections begins with understanding how e-content and the supporting technologies have evolved. Many of the issues that librarians face today can be traced to earlier developments. Understanding the context can inform current choices. This chapter offers an overview of the history of electronic collections and a brief look at the history of the Internet, followed by a synopsis of the issues and challenges that libraries face in developing and managing these collections. These topics are explored in depth in later chapters.

HISTORY OF ELECTRONIC COLLECTIONS

This book makes no claims to offering a comprehensive history of digital collections in libraries, yet a brief introduction to the developments that brought libraries to where they are today seems warranted. Much of the rapid development in electronic collections has occurred in the past five years, but a few dates give a sense of the longer span of development.

Indexes and Abstracting Sources

Medical Literature Analysis and Retrieval System (MEDLARS) was the first on-demand computer-based information retrieval service available to the public, becoming accessible in 1964.[1] MEDLINE, the online version of MEDLARS, and the ERIC (Education Resource Information Center) database followed as the first major remote database search services in 1971. Dialog offered the first online commercial database in 1972. These and other similar services provided online access to the digital versions of print indexes and abstracting services through a dial-up modem. Libraries established searching accounts with these early online database providers, conducted mediated searching, and were charged for connect time. Another option for libraries was acquiring magnetic tapes, loading the tapes locally, and searching from an in-house computer. By the end of the 1970s, more than 360 databases and some forty abstracting and indexing services were available through dial-up access.[2]

Unmediated searching by users became possible in the mid-1980s with the advent of CD-ROMs, which were offered on a subscription basis, often with quarterly or monthly updates, and as an alternative to print indexing and abstracting services. SilverPlatter offered its first CD-ROM databases in 1986.[3] CD-ROMs brought a new business model and complex licensing to libraries. Frequently libraries were required to return the superseded discs to the provider. Some publishers began selling complete versions of print pub-lications, such as encyclopedias, on CD-ROM. Initially CD-ROMs could be accessed by only one user. In the early 1990s cheaper hardware and software solutions allowed simultaneous access of the same CD-ROM database via a local area network. Licenses changed to reflect a specified number of simulta-neous users. Libraries were reluctant to cancel print subscriptions and cease purchasing print because they had limited ability to retain the digital version and few considered CD-ROMs a viable archive or preservation medium.

The shift to remotely hosted e-content paralleled the introduction and growth of the Internet, which is discussed below. By the mid-1990s, numerous providers of CD-ROM databases began offering web-based versions of their content. For example, LexisNexis launched its web-based service for the U.S. legal profession in 1997. The MEDLINE and ERIC databases became avail-able free online the same year. Libraries considering web-based services faced new types of licenses with additional conditions and obligations that needed careful review and negotiation. Issues of perpetual access became more acute because of increasing financial pressures to cancel print even though access to e-content was often limited to the duration of the agreement. Initially, accessing the databases required the use of individual logins and passwords. This awkward approach to authentication was quickly replaced by authentica-tion by Internet Protocol (IP) addresses, with libraries using proxy servers to authenticate remote users. Libraries also faced the challenge of ensuring that their users found the databases to which they had access. Libraries took various approaches to address this, ranging from adding MARC records to the local catalog for these resources to creating online A–Z lists and databases of data-bases—sometimes using all three tactics. Libraries that offered print and elec-tronic versions of the same resource, often with different coverage, faced the challenge of how best to catalog them so readers would find both. Web-based indexes and abstracting services were extremely popular with users in all types of libraries, placing pressure on libraries to resolve this myriad of issues.

One popular addition to web-based indexes and abstracts in the early 2000s was the ability to link to the full-text resources to which the libraries had access. Today, most such resources rely on OpenURLs, which enable the transfer of metadata about an item (e.g., a journal article or book) from a resource where a citation is discovered (e.g., an abstracting and indexing database) to a link resolver.[4] By telling another system what something is rather than where it is located on the Internet (the function of a standard URL), OpenURLs provide a means for link resolvers to direct users to appropriate, subscribed resources for the content. A link resolver is an online utility that uses the OpenURL standard to link between a citation and the electronic full text of the resource cited. The OpenURL linking syntax was developed in 2000, and Ex Libris released the first commercially available link resolver (SFX) 2001.[5]

E-books

The generally accepted birth of the e-book is 1971, when Michael Hart keyed the U.S. Declaration of Independence into a mainframe computer at the University of Illinois.[6] This computer was part of a network that would become the Internet, and Hart's first entry became the genesis of Project Gutenberg (www.gutenberg.org). Initially, these books were downloaded to another computer by File Transfer Protocol (FTP), a network protocol that transfers files from one host to another over a network based on Transmission Control Protocol (TCP). Other collections of free e-books were developed in the 1970s, for example, the Oxford Text Archive in 1976.[7] In the late 1980s companies began to sell books on CD-ROM. Personal users were not enamored with reading books on their computer and generally limited their CD-ROM purchases to reference materials and technical manuals. U.S. libraries began offering online e-books to their users in the mid-1990s through their websites and by linking from records in online catalogs.[8] These e-books tended to be scholarly or technical, had to be viewed on a desktop or laptop computer, and limited the user's ability to download content.

By the mid-1990s society and university presses and commercial publishers were entering the e-book market. Various commercial publishers began developing in-house e-book initiatives through which they could host and sell e-books directly to libraries. Aggregators (e.g., NetLibrary, Questia, and ebrary) begin selling e-book collections to libraries during the same period.

The e-books offered were primarily nonfiction, scholarly, and reference materials designed to be accessed and read on computers and were offered through subscriptions and licensing. Libraries could purchase individual titles and collections of e-books that were hosted on the company's server. Titles were generally limited to one user at a time, and the number of pages that could be printed was also limited. E-textbooks began to appear in the early 2000s.

Initially, fiction e-books were marketed to individuals, but they did not attract a large user base until the appearance of e-book readers that were easy to use, comfortable to hold, and mimicked characteristics of print in their displays. Sony launched the DataDiscman electronic book reader in 1992.[9] Rocket eBook, Cybook, and SoftBook appeared in 1998. Early devices were cumbersome and most people found them unsatisfactory. In 2006 a more powerful generation of readers entered the market with the iRex iLian and the Sony Reader. Amazon's Kindle was introduced in 2007 and Barnes and Noble released the Nook in 2009. Individuals embraced the new e-book readers, and sales of devices and books of all genres took off. Sales figures continue to climb at such a fast pace that relevant statistics are outdated as soon as they are released, but a few data points are indicative of the penetration of e-books and e-book readers. The Pew Research Center reported that, at the end of January 2012, 29 percent of adults in the United States owned at least one tablet or e-book reader.[10] Amazon reported that more than one million Kindle books were available in July 2012.[11] By February 2012, 21 percent of American adults reported that they had read an e-book in the previous year.[12]

Digital rights management (DRM) further complicates the e-book environment. DRM is the technologies used by hardware manufacturers, publishers, and copyright holders to restrict the use of digital content and devices by controlling access to, tracking, and limiting uses of digital works. DRM can limit the devices on which content can be loaded and prevent sharing of content between users even if they have the same type of device. The 1998 Digital Millennium Copyright Act was passed to impose criminal penalties on those who make available technologies intended to circumvent DRM.[13]

Libraries were initially cautious about entering the popular e-book market because of challenges in the compatibility of available books with devices on the market. This changed rapidly. An early company offering e-book collections to libraries was OverDrive, which launched its download service for libraries in 2002 and promises compatibility with all major desktop and mobile platforms. A recent entry (2011) into the market is the 3M Cloud Library. These companies provide customized websites for their library customers. As is the case with most e-content, licenses require careful scrutiny. Because the providers are offering collections from various publishers having multiple authors, titles initially available may be withdrawn from the collection. Nevertheless, many public libraries moved quickly to sign on for this and similar services that permit library users to download content to their own e-book readers or to readers that libraries began to loan to their users.

As the availability of commercial e-books has grown, so too has that of free e-books, with huge numbers made available for downloading or reading online. For example, in July 2012, Project Gutenberg offered more than 40,000 free e-books that could be read online or downloaded as an HTML file, as an EPUB book, or to a Kindle.[14] Of the 20 million books Google had scanned by March 2012, approximately 20 percent are in the public domain and can be read online.[15] Project Gutenberg (a not-for-profit entity) is committed to preserving the content it hosts; many librarians are less confident in perpetual access to Google Books (http://books.google.com). To address this concern, some sixty libraries and research institutions are partnering in HathiTrust (www.hathitrust.org) to ensure long-term curation of scanned content.[16] Anyone can search the HathiTrust Digital Library, but full viewing and downloading of public domain materials are limited to HathiTrust partners. Some free e-books suffer from lack of quality control. Whether to direct users to these resources and, if so, which ones and how to do so are decisions each library must make on the basis of its own mission and user community.

E-books are now pervasive in libraries. A 2012 survey by *Library Journal* found that 89 percent of public libraries in the United States were offering access to e-books, that 90 percent of public library e-book borrowers were reading these on e-book readers, and that 20 percent of public libraries loaned e-readers.[17] Not all research findings agree. *American Libraries'* summer 2012 study reported that 76 percent of public libraries offered e-books and 39 percent loaned e-readers.[18] Another *Library Journal* survey that explored user behavior and preferences reported in October 2011 that 77 percent of library e-book patrons wanted to see more e-books available at their libraries.[19] E-books continue to increase in school libraries and media centers.[20] In 2012, 40 percent of school libraries offered e-books. The higher the grade, the more likely school libraries were to provide e-books, with 63 percent of high school libraries, 50 percent of middle schools, and 33 percent of elementary schools offering them in 2011. Of the 60 percent of school libraries without e-books, 26 percent reported plans to purchase them during the next two years. Not surprisingly, the *Library Journal* study of academic libraries found that 95 percent offered e-books.[21] However, 75 percent of academic library users were still using personal laptops or computers to read e-books. Further, 58 percent of academic library users said they used a library computer to read e-books.

Digital audiobooks (a subset of e-books, sometimes called audio e-books) can be downloaded to desktop and laptop computers and portable devices, depending on the media format and device compatibility. They entered a market dominated by books on cassette and, more recently, books on CD. Many of the commercial providers of e-books to libraries also offer digital audiobooks. One common format is Windows Media Audio (WMA), an audio file format developed by Microsoft. WMA audio e-books are generally compatible with portable devices that support DRM-protected WMA files encoded at a bit rate of 32 kbps. MP3 is another familiar digital audio encoding format, initially used primarily for music (e.g., with iPods) and soon also used for digital audiobooks. MP3 files are compatible with many devices, including most cell phones, personal digital assistants, and MP3 players. WMA audio e-books are about half the file size of MP3 audio e-books but maintain the same level of audio quality. Data released by the Pew Research Center's Internet and American Library Project in early April 2012 reported that 61 percent of audiobook listeners prefer to borrow audiobooks from libraries instead of purchasing them.[22] Digital audiobooks have a special role meeting the needs of the print-impaired.

E-journals and Other Continuing Resources

New Horizons in Adult Education became the first peer-reviewed journal distributed via the Internet, in 1987.[23] It was in ASCII text, free, and sent via an electronic mailing list. However, most early e-serials were not peer-reviewed and tended to be newsletters and other shorter publications with limited graphics. With the introduction of the Internet, e-journals proliferated. Initially, they tended to be issued both in print and electronically. The 1991 edition of the *Directory of Electronic Journals, Newsletters and Academic Discussion Lists* listed twenty-seven e-journals, of which seven were peer-reviewed.[24] By 2000 the directory had narrowed its focus to scholarly resources and listed 3,195 peer-reviewed e-journals, a 560 percent increase in nine years.[25] By 2004, Cole estimated the number of e-journals at 30,000.[26] In August 2012, Ulrichsweb: Global Serials Directory reported 89,888 active online titles.

One important development in journal publication since the early 1990s is open access, the practice of providing unrestricted online access. In Gold OA, a peer-reviewed journal article is made available by the publisher to whom it was submitted. In Green OA, authors self-archive their work in an institutional or discipline-based digital repository or on a personal website. Researchers determined that 191,851 Gold OA articles were published in 2009—a 24.7 percent increase over the previous year—and 4,767 journals were open access in 2009.[27] These numbers continue to increase. By August 2012, the Directory of Open Access Journals (www.doaj.org) listed more than 8,000 peer-reviewed, full-text open-access journals.[28]

Some publishers provide access to journals through their own Internet platforms. Others make their journals available through third-party platforms, such as Project MUSE and Highwire Press. Providing bibliographic access to e-journals (i.e., making them discoverable) created problems for libraries similar to those associated with indexing and abstracting. Libraries used familiar solutions—A–Z lists and MARC records in the local catalog. Helping users find resources in the library was a concern because some users started their search at the publisher's or provider's website, where they were presented with the need to purchase the content without realizing that their local library might offer the resource to affiliated users through a licensing agreement.

E-journals brought familiar licensing issues—controlling access, defining appropriate use, licensor and licensee obligations, terms of the license and fees, and perpetual access. Pricing and business models evolved as the e-journal market expanded. Many publishers began by offering online access free with a print subscription. Others charged an increased price for print-plus-online or a reduced price for print-only or online-only journals. Some publishers offered discounted or special pricing for libraries that purchased large bundled packages of journals (often with multiyear agreements), known as the Big Deal. Smaller libraries often could not afford these packages. Some larger libraries backed away from Big Deals because the packages often included low-usage titles that did not justify the overall cost. Another option is pay-per-view, sometimes called "pay by the drink," in which either the library or the individual pays for the article. Libraries often take this approach if they believe that the total costs of articles from a title in one year will be less than the cost of the annual subscription. E-journal aggregators, third parties that combine the full text of journals from multiple publishers with a common interface or search engine, began marketing their packages to libraries. As is the situation with e-book aggregators, the content is not necessarily stable, further complicating the decision about cancelling the print equivalent of titles in the package.

Managing acquisition information, access provisions, and license conditions became critical as libraries' collections of e-journals grew. In response, libraries developed in-house electronic resources management (ERM) systems. Commercial products, some stand-alone and others incorporated into a vendor's integrated library system (ILS), followed quickly. Innovative Interfaces released the first commercial ERM product in 2003.[29] Serials subscription agents now also offer ERM services. In-house and commercial ERM systems have a common purpose to manage workflow and present the resource name and associated information about licensing restrictions and obligations; supplier, subscription cost, and renewal cycle; troubleshooting and other contact information; whether the title is part of package; and, more recently, usage data in a single place. ERM systems have expanded to manage all types of e-content and are not limited to e-journals.

E-journals now dominate journal collections in academic and research libraries. The move to general-interest online magazines and newspapers has been slower in all types of libraries for various reasons. Many of these e-publications provide free access to their online content, although some publishers require a subscription fee to access "premium" articles or to retrieve from backfiles. Many online magazines and newspapers that provide free access generate revenue through banner ads, affiliations with retail websites, classified ads, and other sources that subsidize the e-content (or generate a profit). Newspaper and magazine publishers entered the market by targeting their e-versions to individual consumers, especially those with personal e-readers.

As library users came to expect access to other types of e-content, some expressed interest in public libraries providing access to newspapers and general-interest magazines. Simultaneously, subscription agents entered the market by offering to package and manage subscriptions for these types of materials, but not the premium subscription versions marketed to individuals. Many public libraries that offer e-journal and e-magazines do so through regional and state agreements. For the most part, library patron access to this e-content is via a computer and not reader devices, but the marketplace is changing rapidly. McPheters and Co. estimates that half of all magazine and newspaper circulation will be via digital delivery by the end of 2015.[30]

Multimedia

Libraries that acquired and circulated phonograph records and cassettes started circulating audio CDs when they began to dominate the music industry in the late 1980s. Libraries followed a similar path as the distribution of movies for home viewing switched from video cassettes and video discs to DVDs. Streaming audio, distributed in real time over the Internet, became more widely available with the development of consumer-oriented software such as RealAudio, the first audio streaming solution developed for the Internet, by RealNetworks in 1995. Audio was the initial e-content delivered as streaming media. The music library at the University of California–Berkeley began streaming music course reserves soon thereafter and the UCB Media Resources Center entered into its first digital audio project with the Pacifica Radio Foundation.[31]

Streaming video took longer than streaming audio to become widely available. Reasons for the delay were the need for sufficient processing power in home computers and network bandwidth to support the required data rates, pervasive access to the Internet, and implementation of standard protocols and formats. Although multimedia software was available—Apple's Quick-Time, a multimedia framework that can handle various formats of digital sound, video, and still images was released in 1991, and Microsoft Windows 3.0 included multimedia extensions in the same year—the market was dependant on home computers and bandwidth able to handle the content. The mid-1990s saw a convergence of solutions. Adobe Flash Player, a now pervasive software for viewing multimedia and streaming video and audio, was released in 1996. The Library of Congress took advantage of advances in technology and the Internet and began making digitized collections (piloted in the early 1990s on CD-ROMs) available as streaming media beginning with the American Memory project in the mid-1990s.[32] YouTube, which uploaded its first video in April 2005, introduced many computer users to streaming multimedia.[33] One of the early providers of digital video delivery to schools, higher education institutions, and public libraries was Films On Demand, which was established in 2005 one month after YouTube launched.[34] Library investment in digital video accessed online or streamed in public and academic libraries remains a modest portion of expenditures. Primary Research Group reported in 2011 that only 1 percent of total video expenditures in public libraries was spent on streaming video, compared to 15.1 percent in academic libraries.[35]

As institutional consumers of on-demand multimedia, libraries and schools are participating in a market that is evolving in terms of both content and economic models—and certainly licensing models. At this point, most streaming video available to libraries and schools consists of educational content and documentaries offered by distributors who specialize in these types of materials. As Handman points out, on-demand delivery of theatrical feature films is geared to mass-market, pay-per-view sales, and the future of institutional licensing for mass-marketed titles is uncertain.[36] Media distributors, similar to e-book distributors, are subject to the arrangements made with the creators and other owners of the intellectual property. Terms of access are generally limited to five years or less, and renewals depend on the distributors' arrangements with the filmmaker. The issues facing libraries desiring to offer streaming media to their users remain complex.

INTERNET AND THE WEB

The history of electronic collections must be considered in the context of the Internet. The origin of the Internet is traced to the Advanced Research Projects Agency Network (ARPANet), created in the 1960s and 1970s by the U.S. Department of Defense to link military, research, and academic computer centers. Over time, the network expanded, but it did not start becoming a global system until a 1990 proposal by Tim Berners-Lee, then working with the European Organization for Nuclear Research (CERN) and now director of the World Wide Web Consortium (W3C), developed the idea of a system of interlinked hyptertext documents accessed by the Internet. He developed the tools and standard protocols and formats required for a working web. These included Hypertext Transfer Protocol (HTTP), Hypertext Markup Language (HTML), the first web browser, the first HTTP server software, the first web server, and the first web pages, which described the project itself. The initial goal was to allow high-energy physicists to share information easily and quickly.

The Mosaic web browser, developed by Marc Andreessen and a team of programmers at the University of Illinois at Urbana–Champaign, was released in 1993 and opened the Web to everyone.[37] It was one of the first browsers to use a multimedia graphic interface and was both free and easy to download and install. Hudson notes the explosion in the growth ("hovering around tens of thousands of percent over ridiculously short periods") of the Web after Mosaic was introduced.[38]

People tend to use the terms Internet and World Wide Web (or simply the Web) synonymously, but they are not the same. The Internet is the worldwide system of interconnected computer networks. The Web is the global set of documents, images, and other resources, related by hyperlinks and referenced with uniform resource identifiers (URIs). URIs identify services, servers, other databases, and the documents and resources they can provide. HTTP is the main access protocol of the Web. Web services also use HTTP to allow software systems to communicate in order to share and exchange business logic and data. Browser software, such as Internet Explorer and Google Chrome, lets users navigate from one web page to another via hyperlinks embedded in the documents. These documents also may contain combinations of data, including graphics, sounds, text, video, multimedia, and interactive content that run while the user is interacting with the page. Search engines such as Yahoo! and Google, which use keyword searching to "crawl" the Web, give users access to online information worldwide.

The Internet is heavily used by all ages. According to Internet World Stats, use of the Internet increased worldwide by 566.4 percent between 2000 and 2012.[39] In 2012, 78.6 percent of the population of North America and 34.3 percent of the world's population were using the Internet. In 2011 the Pew Research Center reported that 35 percent of Americans owned smartphones and that 52 percent of those between the ages of 18 and 29 owned them.[40] Further, 68 percent of smartphone owners used them to go online on a typical day. Mobile phones have moved from primarily a means of communication to a means of accessing content. The Internet and computing technology have driven the growth of e-content in libraries by reshaping how content is accessed, delivered, and managed. The pervasiveness of the Internet, computers, and mobile devices coupled with the publication of vast amounts of information on the Web have made developing electronic collections essential for libraries.

CHALLENGES

Many of the challenges libraries face in developing and managing electronic collections are similar to those inherent in developing and managing any type of content, but many others are not. In addition, the issues surrounding e-resources are constantly changing. At the core of addressing these challenges is the need to provide users with a unified information environment, reduce their confusion, and meet their expectations for convenience and simplicity.

E-content presents libraries with seemingly endless choices. It can be born digital or digitized from nondigital information, can be held locally or accessed on a remote server, is available in a range of file formats, spans genres, and comes as individual titles or packaged in collections. It can be read on conventional computers or mobile devices or downloaded to handheld readers. Making informed decisions can feel like chasing information on the Web—each decision leads to the need for additional choices. The first and

MOBILE DEVICES

E-book readers are mobile or portable electronic devices designed for the purpose of reading e-content. Because e-book readers are designed for reading, their screens offer better readability, especially in bright sunlight, and longer battery life. E-readers use display technologies (electronic paper, e-paper, e-ink) that mimic the appearance of ink on paper. Unlike conventional backlit displays that emit light, electronic paper displays reflect light like ordinary paper.

Personal digital assistants (PDAs) are handheld devices that combine computing, telephone, Internet, and networking features.

Smartphones are mobile phones with advanced computing ability and connectivity. They combine multiple functions with the ability to make phone calls. They often can serve as web browsers, media players, digital cameras, video cameras, and GPS navigation units. Smartphones have advanced application programming interfaces (APIs) that can run third-party applications (apps).

Tablet computers, also called simply tablets, are mobile computers. They are larger than mobile phones or PDAs. Tablets are integrated into a flat touch screen and primarily operated by touching the screen rather than using a physical keyboard. A tablet computer typically has a faster screen capable of higher refresh rates than e-book readers, making them more suitable for interaction.

obvious decision is whether an e-version is the best solution to providing the content, yet even this requires carefully comparing options and user needs and expectations within the context of the library's mission.

Part of the decision making requires understanding the business models in play, with the associated pricing and licensing options. Nearly all fee-based e-content requires a license. Reviewing and negotiating licenses require attention to detail and understanding licensing terms, conditions, and library obligations. Purchase transfers ownership to the library and ensures perpetual access, but it can place the onus on the library to curate and provide access to the content. Subscriptions may be annual or longer, but they have a fixed term and may or may not include perpetual access. Some licenses for e-journals place a cap on annual increases, others do not. Understanding pricing and licensing options and what is negotiable is essential.

Another aspect of each business model that must be scrutinized is the content provided. Much e-content comes bundled, either in publisher packages or collections assembled by e-content aggregators. Packages of titles may include content of little interest to the library, yet the package may cost less than the total of individual titles in which a library is interested. Aggregators of titles from various publishers often cannot guarantee content stability, which has implications for long-term access. This can be especially disquieting when a library is making choices about what to retain in print. Knowing what content is being offered, how the provider decides what to include, and when and how content is added and removed requires careful assessment.

DRM technology of some type is present in nearly all e-content that libraries pay to access or acquire. The limitations on use of digital content and devices inherent in DRM are sometimes called *hard restrictions* because they strictly prevent specific uses. DRM often supplements the restrictions mandated in licenses. The use of DRM remains controversial, with proponents and opponents on both sides. The future of DRM in law and practice warrants monitoring.

In addition to determining what a particular e-resource costs initially and projecting (to the extent possible) future increases, a library should make selection decisions within the context of institutional financial considerations. Libraries generally have been focused on keeping allocations and expenditures for books and serials balanced to avoid annual serials expenditures consuming too much of the book budget. This balancing act has become more complicated because access to much e-content also is provided through annual subscriptions. Projecting continuing commitments now requires understanding all long-term financial obligations regardless of the type of content being delivered.

Ensuring equity of access is of vital importance as libraries move increasingly to digital content. Equity of access means that everyone a library serves has access to the library resources they need and does not face barriers because of age, education, ethnicity, language, income, physical limitations, or geographic location. The rapid growth of e-content has led to increased concern over difficulties faced by users without ready access to computers, e-readers, or other mobile devices; users with physical limitations; and remote users. Libraries should take care to ensure that these users have the same level of access to resources.

Increasing amounts of digital content in libraries present new challenges for technical services staff who process and make the material discoverable.

E-content must be licensed and activated in OpenURL knowledge bases. Metadata to facilitate discovery must be created or acquired. Many vendors and publishers do not provide metadata for the content in the packages they sell; in other cases, the metadata they offer do not meet the quality standards set by libraries. Libraries must make choices about which data points are most critical for discovery and need to be upgraded.

Libraries are developing new workflow models for managing e-content. Many libraries find that the tasks of acquiring, licensing, activating, and describing these resources require more time and effort and a higher level of staff than the tasks associated with traditional resources. ERM systems are helping, but these must be either developed locally or acquired, then populated with the necessary information. Because many ERM systems depend on the accuracy and currency of a knowledge base, a complete and reliable knowledge base is essential. Many technical standards exist and have eased technical service processes, but local issues often mean that libraries handle workflow differently. Management and delivery of e-content continue to challenge technical services and other units involved in selecting and making e-content discoverable and accessible.

E-content collection development and management take on additional complexities beyond selecting the best resource. Collection policies must reflect the variety of formats and may include policy decisions addressing preferred formats and conditions for selecting the e-version of a resource. Decisions about adding e-content are often made in cooperation with other libraries in consortia. Collection maintenance (decisions about weeding and storage, cancellation, archiving, and preservation) takes on new nuances in the e-content environment. Use statistics, a familiar tool for informed collection maintenance decisions, for e-content are seldom reflected in circulation systems. Other means of tracking use and user satisfaction are necessary. Relying on vendor-supplied use data is increasingly important, but this is complicated by a need for meaningful comparative data. Collection development and management have always been both art and science—and both are more demanding in the digital collections environment.

The increasing amount of e-content that libraries own and to which they provide access has complicated the user discovery experience. Traditional online catalogs and A–Z journal and database lists are no longer sufficient. Next-generation catalogs provide new discovery layers, unyoked from the underlying ILS. They offer advantages through increased intuitive functionality and interfaces that are more user-friendly. However, the user experience is not seamless. Next-generation catalogs still rely on link resolvers to select the appropriate e- content provider, and users often must search again for the specific source they seek. Web-scale discovery services are the newest attempt to simplify the user discovery and access experience. Web-scale discovery services allow users to search quickly and seamlessly in a single intuitive interface across an immense array of local and remote preharvested and indexed content and provide the relevancy-ranked results that users expect. The first of these services appeared in late 2007, and most currently available services were released in 2010. All are evolving rapidly.

An overview of the challenges before libraries is not complete without a note on the effects of evolving technologies on user expectations. Increasing computing power in devices of all types, pervasiveness of the Internet in daily life, and ubiquity of e-readers, tablets, and smartphones compel libraries to monitor these areas to meet the evolving needs and expectations of their user communities. E-content discovery and delivery systems must interact with a variety of search tools and technologies. Supporting mobile access to all types of e-content (from books to databases to audio and video) is an opportunity that libraries cannot ignore in their goal of offering users a seamless search and access experience.

SUMMARY

Electronic collections are the digital content selected by librarians for a library, managed by the library, and made available for users. The history of e-content in libraries goes back more than fifty years, but the current era can be traced to the mid-1980s, when much of the e-content acquired or leased by libraries was in the form of CD-ROMs, accessed by computers within the library. Some content was available through FTP over the Internet. Release of the first free and easy-to-download Internet browser in 1993 spurred general public use of the Internet and led commercial content providers to offer their products to libraries as online resources. These early resources were frequently indexing and abstracting databases and reference tools. The number of e-journals began to increase rapidly in the late 1990s.

Although e-books have been available online since the 1970s, widespread e-book provision by libraries began in the mid-1990s when providers marketed titles that were read on computers and could not be downloaded. Streaming multimedia in libraries followed a decade later. E-books and streaming media took off in libraries with the arrival of devices that met user expectations in ease of use and affordability.

Regardless of format and access and delivery mechanisms, e-content presents challenges for libraries in selection, business models, pricing and licensing options, fiscal planning, collection management, and workflow. Ensuring equity of access without barriers for any member of the user community is an ongoing concern. Constantly evolving technologies and the popularity of mobile devices further challenge libraries. Building an e-collection is an ongoing process. Identifying, evaluating, selecting, and licensing e-resources are the first steps. E-resources also must be made discoverable and accessible, managed, and maintained.

Suggested Readings

Anson, Catherine, and Ruth R. Connell. *E-book Collections.* SPEC Kit 313. Washington, DC: Association of Research Libraries, 2009.

Brown, David J., and Richard Boulderstone. *The Impact of Electronic Publishing: The Future for Publishers and Librarians.* Munich: G. K. Saur, 2008.

Brumley, Rebecca. *Electronic Collection Management: Forms, Policies, Procedures, and Guidelines Manual with CD-ROM.* New York: Neal-Schuman, 2009.

Buczynski, James A. "The Library Patron Prefers Listening: Living in Ray Bradbury's Personal Audio Universe." *Internet Reference Services Quarterly* 11, no. 2 (2006): 97–103.

Chief Officers of State Library Agencies. "COSLA: eBook Feasibility Study for Public Libraries; Final Report" (June 30, 2010). www.cosla.org/documents/COSLA2270_Report_Final1.pdf.

Clement, Susanne K., and Jennifer M. Foy. *Collection Development in a Changing Environment: Policies and Organization for College and University Libraries.* Chicago: Association of College and Research Libraries, 2010.

Collins, Maria D. D., and Patrick L. Carr, eds. *Managing the Transition from Print to Electronic Journals and Resources: A Guide for Library and Information Professionals.* New York: Routledge, 2008.

Davis, Denise M. "E-books: Collection Vortex or Black Hole?" *Public Libraries* 49, no. 4 (2010): 10–53.

Doi, Carolyn, James Mason, and Jared Wiercinski. "Mobile Access to Audio and Video Collections in Libraries and Other Cultural Institutions." *Partnership: The Canadian Journal of Library and Information Practice and Research* 6, no. 1 (2011). http://journal.lib.uoguelph .ca/index.php/perj/article/viewArticle/1246/1987.

"E-content: The Digital Dialogue." E-content Supplement to *American Libraries* (May/June 2012). http://viewer.zmags.com/publication/f8ac9caa.

Eschenfelder, Kristin R. "Every Library's Nightmare? Digital Rights Management, Use Restrictions, and Licensed Scholarly Digital Resources." *College and Research Libraries* 69, no. 3 (June 2008): 205–25.

Guernsey, Lisa. "Are Ebooks Any Good? Do Digital Books Help Young Kids Learn to Read, or Are They Mostly Fun and Games?" *School Library Journal* 57, no. 6 (June 2011): 28–32.

Hawthorne, Darlene. "History of Electronic Resources." In *Electronic Resource Management in Libraries: Research and Practice,* ed. Holly Yu and Scott Breivold, 1–15. Hershey, PA: Information Science Reference, 2008.

Horava, Tony. "Challenges and Possibilities for Collection Management in a Digital Age." *Library Resources and Technical Services* 54, no. 3 (July 2010): 142–52.

Ivins, October, ed. "Views of the E-books Renaissance." Special edition of *ISQ: Information Standards Quarterly* 23, no. 2 (Spring 2011).

Joint eBooks Reader Committee [Poudre River Public Library District, Colorado State University, Front Range Community College]. "eBooks and eReaders in Public and Academic Libraries." May 2011. www.poudrelibraries.org/about/pdf/ereader-report-2011extended.pdf.

Lee, Jane. "E-books: Understanding the Basics." June 2009. www.cdlib.org/inside/assess/evaluation_activities/docs/2009/e-book_basics_june2009.pdf.

Lightman, Harriet, and John P. Bloser, eds. *Perspectives on Serials in the Hybrid Environment*. ACLTS Papers on Library Technical Services and Collections 15. Chicago: American Library Association, 2007.

PricewaterhouseCoopers. *Turning the Page: The Future of eBooks*. 2010. www.pwc.com/en_GX/gx/entertainment-media/pdf/eBooks-Trends-Developments.pdf.

Raine, Lee, et al. *The Rise of E-reading*. Washington, DC: Pew Internet and American Life Project, 2012. http://libraries.pewinternet.org/files/legacy-pdf/The%20rise%200f%20e-reading%204.5.12.pdf.

Roxburgh, Stephen. "The E-future." *Horn Book Magazine* 88, no. 2 (Mar./Apr. 2012): 10–21.

Spiro, Lisa, and Geneva Henry. "Can a New Research Library Be All-Digital?" In *The Idea of Order: Transforming Research Collections for 21st Century Scholarship*, 5–80. CLIR Publication 147. Washington, DC: Council on Library and Information Resources, 2010.

Webster, Peter M. *Managing Electronic Resources: New and Changing Roles for Libraries*. Oxford, UK: Chandos, 2008.

Wikoff, Karin. *Electronic Resources Management in the Academic Library: A Professional Guide*. Santa Barbara, CA: Libraries Unlimited, 2012.

Yelton, Adromada. "Ebooks Choices and the Soul of Librarianship." *The Digital Shift* (July 30, 2012), www.thedigitalshift.com/2012/07/ebooks/ebooks-choices-and-the-soul-of-librarianship.

Zickuhr, Kathryn, et al. *Libraries, Patrons, and E-books*. Washington, DC: Pew Internet and American Life Project, 2012. http://libraries.pewinternet.org/files/legacy-pdf/PIP_Libraries_and_Ebook_Patrons%206.22.12.pdf.

Notes

1. Sharon A. Weiner, "Tale of Two Databases: The History of Federally Funded Information Systems for Education and Medicine," *Government Information Quarterly* 26, no. 3 (2009): 450–58.

2. Roger W. Christian, *The Electronic Library: Bibliographic Data Bases, 1978–1979* (White Plains, NY: Knowledge Industry Publications, 1978).

3. FundingUniverse, "SilverPlatter Information Inc.," www.fundinguniverse.com/company-histories/SilverPlatter-Information-Inc-Company-History.html.

4. James Culling, *Link Resolvers and the Serials Supply Chain: Final Project Report for UKSG* (Oxford, UK: Scholarly Information Strategies, 2007), www.uksg.org/sites/uksg.org/files/uksg_link_resolvers_final_report.pdf.

5. National Information Standards Organization, *The OpenURL Framework for Context-*

Sensitive Services, ANSI/NISO Z39.88–2004 (Bethesda, Maryland: NISO, 2005) defines the architecture for creating the OpenURL framework.

6. William Grimes, "Michael Hart, A Pioneer of E-books, Dies at 64," *New York Times* (Sept. 8, 2011), www.nytimes.com/2011/09/09/business/michael-hart-a-pioneer-of-e-books-dies -at-64.html.

7. Oxford University Computing Services, "Frequently Asked Questions of the Oxford Text Archive," http://ota.ahds.ac.uk/about/faq.xml.

8. Doris Small, "E-books in Libraries: Some Early Experiences and Reactions," *Searcher* 8, no. 9 (2000): 63–65.

9. Michael Coburn et al., "Ebook Readers: Directions in Enabling Technologies," in *Print and Electronic Text Convergence,* ed. Bill Cope and Diana Kalantzis, 145–82 (Melbourne: Common Ground, 2001).

10. Lee Rainier, *Tablet and E-book Reader Ownership Nearly Double over the Holiday Gift-Giving Period* (Washington, DC: Pew Research Center, 2012), www.pewinternet.org/~/media//Files/ Reports/2012/Pew_Tablets%20and%20e-readers%20double%201.23.2012.pdf.

11. Amazon.com, "Kindle for PC," www.amazon.com/gp/feature.html?ie=UTF8&docId=100042 6311&tag=googhydr-20&hvadid=7893047648&ref=pd_sl_3ies3d4yuc_b.

12. Lee Rainier et al., *The Rise of E-reading* (Washington, DC: Pew Research Center Internet and American Libraries Project, 2012), http://libraries.pewinternet.org/files/legacy-pdf/The%20 rise%200f%20e-reading%204.5.12.pdf.

13. *The Digital Millennium Copyright Act,* 105th Cong., 2d sess. (1998).

14. Project Gutenberg News, "Project Gutenberg 40,000th eBook Milestone" (July 8, 2012), www .gutenbergnews.org.

15. Jennifer Howard, "Google Begins to Scale Back Its Scanning of Books from University Libraries," *Chronicle of Higher Education* (Mar. 9, 2012), http://chronicle.com/article/Google -Begins-to-Scale-Back/131109.

16. Heather Christenson, "HathiTrust: A Research Library at Web Scale," *Library Resources and Technical Services* 55, no. 2 (Apr. 2011): 93–102; Jeremy York, "HathiTrust: The Elephant in the Library," *Library Issues* 32, no. 3 (Jan. 2012): 1–5.

17. *Ebook Usage in U.S. Public Libraries, Third Annual Survey* (New York: Library Journal, 2012).

18. American Libraries, *Public Library Funding and Technology Access Study 2011–2012, American Libraries Digital Supplement* (Summer 2012), www.ala.org/research/plftas/2011_2012.

19. Steve Paxhia and John Parsons, "Library Patrons and Ebook Usage Analysis," *Library Journal Patron Profiles* 1, no. 1 (Oct. 2011).

20. *Ebook Usage in U.S. School (K–12) Libraries, Third Annual Survey* (New York: Library Journal, 2012).

21. *Ebook Usage in U.S. Academic Libraries, Third Annual Survey* (New York: Library Journal, 2012).

22. Rainer et al., *Rise of E-reading.*

23. *New Horizons in Adult Education* 1, no. 1(Fall 1987).

24. *Directory of Electronic Journals, Newsletters, and Academic Discussion Lists* (Washington, DC: Association of Research Libraries, Office of Scholarly Communication, 1991).

25. *Directory of Scholarly Electronic Journals and Academic Discussion Lists* (Washington, DC: Association of Research Libraries, Office of Scholarly Communication, 2000).

26. Louise Cole, "Back to Basics: What Is the E-journal?" *Serials Librarian* 47, no. 1/2 (2004): 77–87.

27. Mikael Laakso et al., "The Development of Open Access Journal Publishing from 1993 to 2009," *PLoS One* 6, no. 6 (June 2011), www.plosone.org/article/info%3Adoi%2F10.1371%2Fjournal .pone.0020961.

28. Total of journals from The DOAJ: Directory of Open Access Journals website, www.doaj.org; see also Heather Morrison, "Happy 2012 Open Access Movement! December 31, 2011 Dramatic Growth of Open Access," *Imaginary Journal of Poetic Economics,* Dec. 31, 2011. http:// poeticeconomics.blogspot.com/2011/12/happy-2012-open-access-movement.html.

29. Diane Grover and Theodore Fons, "The Innovative Electronic Resource Management System: A Development Partnership," *Serials Librarian* 30, no. 2 (2004): 110–16.

30. Rebecca McPheters, "Magazines and Newspapers Need to Build Better Apps" (Jan. 13, 2012), *Ad Age Mediaworks,* http://adage.com/article/mediaworks/viewpoint-magazines-newspapers -build-apps/232085.

31. Gary Handman, Media Resources Center, Moffitt Library, University of California, Berkeley, e-mail to the author, Jan. 30, 2012.

32. Library of Congress, American Memory, "About American Memory," http://memory.loc.gov/ ammem/about.

33. YouTube, "Timeline," www.youtube.com/t/press_timeline.

34. Wendy Collins, vice president, Films Media Group, e-mail to author, Jan. 31, 2012.

35. Primary Research Group, *Library Use of Video and Audio* (New York: Primary Research Group, 2011).

36. Gary Handman, "License to Look: Evolving Models for Library Video Acquisition and Access," *Library Trends* 58, no. 3 (Winter 2010): 324–34.

37. NCSA, About NCSA Mosaic, www.ncsa.illinois.edu/Projects/mosaic.html.

38. David Hudson, *Rewired: A Brief and Opinionated Net History* (Indianapolis: Macmillan Technical Publishing, 1970), 42.

39. Internet World Stats, "Usage and Population Statistics," www.internetworldstats.com/stats .htm.

40. Aaron Smith, *35% of American Adults Own a Smartphone* (Washington, DC: Pew Research Center, 2011), http://pewinternet.org/Reports/2011/Smartphones.aspx.

CHAPTER 2

SELECTING AND EVALUATING E-RESOURCES FOR LIBRARIES

THIS CHAPTER EXPLORES selection and management of e-resources from the perspective of those responsible for these tasks. The lines between the types of e-resources available to libraries are blurring, and many similar decisions apply regardless of type of content. This chapter addresses key decision points and criteria that guide choices for all types of e-content and concludes with an examination of the components of making the decision to cancel or remove an e-resource.

SELECTION CRITERIA

The most basic guideline for selecting e-content is to choose content that meets user needs and advances the mission of the library, but making that decision involves several considerations. These considerations are most effectively addressed in a collections policy or policies, which can both serve as a resource for library staff and inform users. A collections policy likely spells out general selection criteria and perhaps those specific to e-resources. Some libraries also have supplemental sections or policies addressing e-resources. These might cover such topics as how the library handles licenses (who negotiates them, who has authority to sign them, etc.) and services, conditions, and clauses that are required. The latter may apply to any aspect of the license, from a mandated definition of authorized users to no restrictions on interlibrary loan (ILL) to a guarantee of perpetual access. If a library is moving toward e-preferred as a replacement for print, this section or supplemental policy explains the conditions that must be met to acquire the e-content in lieu of print.

The basic criteria that librarians apply when selecting resources remain for the most part constant, regardless of the medium of delivery. These include[1]

- content or subject
- cost
- language
- currency
- veracity
- writing style (e.g., well written, easy to read, aesthetic aspects)
- completeness and scope of treatment
- reputation, credentials, or authoritativeness of author, publisher, editor, reviewers
- geographic coverage
- quality of scholarship
- relation to curriculum and learning outcomes
- frequency the title is referenced in bibliographies or citations
- reading or user level to which content is directed
- comprehensiveness and breadth
- frequency of updates or revisions
- access points (e.g., indexes, level of detail in the table of contents)
- ease of use
- external resources that index the publication
- physical quality (e.g., illustrations, paper and binding, format, typography, durability, visual and audio characteristics)
- uniqueness of content, capabilities, or features
- availability of equipment required for hearing or viewing audiovisual material

Not all criteria apply to all items or to all categories of materials, and additional criteria may apply to some formats, such as the quality of art in children's books.

E-resources have additional criteria that guide their selection. These include consideration of

- provider business model
- persistency of content
- functionality of the user interface
- ease of authentication
- accessibility
- local service implications and local physical and logistical requirements
- OpenURL compliance

- output options
- compatibility with e-readers and other mobile devices
- duplication or replacement of existing library resources
- availability of data to measure use and effectiveness
- availability of descriptive metadata for local use
- licensing and contractual terms, limitations, and obligations

Currency of e-books has an added aspect because many publishers delay release of the e-book version of a title until after the print version has been available for a period of time. Libraries should be attentive to this if they make decisions about e-preferred instead of preference for print books.

Provider Business Model

According to Amit and Zott, "A business model depicts the content, structure, and governance of transactions designed so as to create value through the exploitation of business opportunities."[2] The business models used by e-content providers define what they create and deliver, conditions of delivery and access, and how they generate revenue. Content providers can be publishers, vendors, aggregators and other agents, and even individuals. Providers aim for business models that generate revenue, protect content from piracy, and appeal to libraries. The variability of business models challenges librarians as they seek content that matches local needs and expectations at an affordable price.

Publishers offer access to their own publications, which may be journals, books, or other formats. Vendors are suppliers through which libraries obtain books, serials, other materials, and services instead of dealing directly with a publisher. Many vendors offer both print books and e-books. Agents are companies that act as intermediaries between a library and a publisher, such as subscription agents or book vendors. Aggregators are third-party providers that combine the full text of journals, articles, or books originally published by multiple publishers with a common interface or search engine and generally offer e-content in packages.

Business models have various elements, all of which merit consideration. One important decision point is whether the library is paying to access the content for a period of time (e.g., subscribing to a journal or a package of e-content for a year) or purchasing the content (e.g., purchasing journal back-files or e-books). Both are governed by licenses. If the library enters into an annual contract or subscription for access, another point for consideration is whether the library owns the content to which it subscribed for the term of the subscription. Usually, the answer is no, but this may be addressed in the license agreement.

In addition to the obvious consideration of initial cost, most e-content carries a continuing financial commitment to renew the license and, if applicable, the service agreement. Some providers offer pricing caps—a promise not to increase the yearly cost more than a set percentage annually—if the library commits to a multiyear subscription. In some cases this cap is contingent on not reducing expenditures. In other words, the provider guarantees to limit price increases if the library agrees not to cancel journal titles or reduce the number of books purchased. Big Deals, the large bundled packages of journals from a single publisher, provided in a multiyear agreement, have been debated since they were first offered. Some libraries find them cost effective and appreciate the expanded title access; others are unhappy that they are paying for lesser-used journals and do not find the overall cost justified. Popular with consortia, Big Deals protect the publishers' revenue stream by extending the length of the contract and restricting cancellations. One aspect that libraries can find attractive is that Big Deals offers predictability of pricing for the duration of the agreement.

Cost also varies according to the business model. Access-based pricing is determined by the number of simultaneous users for which the library contracts. Beyond that maximum, prospective users are turned away. Site licenses provide for unlimited users and are based on the number of potential users (e.g., FTE students, faculty, and staff; number of researchers; citizens in a county). They may be further limited by geographic locations, IP addresses, or both. This model is attractive for content that will have high use. Another option is pay-per-view (pay-per-use, pay-by-the-drink), in which either the library or the individual pays for the content. Libraries often take this approach for journals if they believe that the total costs of articles from a title in one year will be less than the cost of the annual subscription. Some e-books are available in a similar pay-per-view model. One appealing aspect of this business model is that it allows an unlimited number of simultaneous users. On the negative side, this model can be difficult for libraries to budget. Libraries either prepay for a block of vouchers or tokens or are billed monthly; funds allocated for this service can be expended quickly. Libraries need to understand clearly the pricing schemes available and their longer-term implications. Choosing the appropriate pricing model is important.

The business model for e-journals, reference resources, and indexing and abstracting resources has stabilized in recent years. Although libraries may not always be satisfied with the options offered, they are generally understood. The business model for e-books is in flux and volatile. Many publishers do not have a clear business model that meets their goals of protecting revenue and intellectual property. Some purchasing models are similar to those for e-journals—pay-per-view, bundled (often subject collections), and patron-driven acquisition in which a title is purchased only when it is accessed (usually a predetermined number of times). Some publishers refuse to make their e-books available for library lending. Others limit access to their own integrated online platform. Some publishers also make their books available through selected vendors and aggregators. Again, this is a dynamic, rapidly changing area. If a library is interested in books from a specific publisher, checking with both the publisher and vendors and aggregators with which the library is already working is advisable.

In addition to explicit lending limitations that publishers may place on their e-books, DRM technology limits the devices on which e-books can be read, further complicating the situation for libraries loaning e-books to patrons. A 2011 survey on digital book publishing by the Association of American University Presses found that 84 percent of respondents were either very interested or interested in new business models.[3] Until publishers settle on a business model for e-books, libraries need to monitor the e-book environment carefully.

DIGITAL RIGHTS MANAGEMENT

DRM technologies give copyright owners control over how digital content and services may be used. These technologies protect electronically accessible material from unauthorized use through software or hardware and establish the circumstances under which users can access the e-content. In addition to controlling simple access to digital materials, DRM can control specific activities (e.g., printing, copying, saving e-content) and can limit the number of times an activity can be performed. A license or some type of key is required to access DRM-controlled content. The controls enforced by DRM technologies can correspond to license terms or be more stringent. As is the case with license terms, DRM can impose limitations on use that do not conform to U.S. copyright law governing fair use of library materials.

Persistency of Content

This criterion has two components: the extent to which e-content remains unchanged during the term of the license, and the provision of permanent access to the e-content after the library terminates the license or the provider stops offering the product or ceases operation. Both areas should be addressed in the license.

Persistency of e-content during the license term is primarily an issue with aggregators, who license content from publishers. Aggregators may offer a package of titles, but often they cannot guarantee that the collections of titles will remain constant. This is a consideration when libraries cancel print journal subscriptions and depend on e-journals in aggregator packages. Publishers can pull titles from packages for various reasons. They may opt to offer a title only through their proprietary websites or fail to reach an acceptable agreement with the aggregator. Some publishers question the extent to which their intellectual property or revenue stream is protected. In fall 2011, Penguin pulled its books from the aggregator OverDrive because OverDrive distributed Penguin's e-books to Amazon's Kindle Lending Library, which did not have a contract with Penguin allowing them to do so. Penguin stated, "Due to new concerns about the security of our digital editions, we find it necessary to delay the availability of our new titles in the digital format while we resolve these concerns with our business partners."[4] Later, Penguin announced that libraries would have continued access to titles to which they already had access, but not to new titles. Furthermore, Penguin e-books loaded for reading on Kindle devices would have to be downloaded to a computer and then transferred to the device over a USB connection, eliminating the convenience of borrowing e-books from a mobile device.

Libraries generally aim for some means of affordable, practical, perpetual, or permanent access to the licensed content. This is related to the issue of whether the library is leasing access during the term of the contract or purchasing the content. A license may grant the library the right to create backup copies for preservation purposes, but this means the library must have an infrastructure in place to host and access the content. In other cases, the content provider makes a commitment to archive content through an entity or service, such as Lots of Copies Keep Stuff Safe (LOCKSS), Controlled LOCKSS (CLOCKSS), Portico, or a trusted third party that has permanent archival responsibility for the resource if the publisher ceases the publication or goes out of business.

In some cases, the library purchases the content and, therefore, owns it in perpetuity. Two models are possible. In one the library acquires the content, mounts it and manages discovery and access locally, and takes responsibility for preserving it. In the other the library purchases the content and pays the provider an annual platform maintenance fee to support ongoing hosting of the e-content and provision of the interface. This can apply to most types of content, from e-books to journal backfiles. Random House's January 2012 announcement that raised the price of its e-books to library aggregators (OverDrive, 3M, Ingram, etc.) stated that, once a library bought a book, it could loan it an unlimited number of times and never have to pay for it again—that is, perpetual ownership.[5]

Functionality of the User Interface

A user interface is the system though which users interact with the content. Libraries and users want an interface that is easy, efficient, and effective. Interfaces are native to resources, generally proprietary, and vary from platform to platform. An interface should be intuitive and provide context-sensitive help screens as well as complete and helpful documentation. The interface should use clear, consistent terminology. Users should be able to determine their status (where they are and where to go next) easily, and the interface should offer easy navigation. This might involve tables of contents and indexes linking to text, ability to page forward and backward, a "jump to" page feature, or a capability to browse the text, table of contents, and index. Viewing and manipulating results should be easy. The interface should offer a spell-check and, ideally, suggest alternatives to misspelled words.

The search options should be self-explanatory, readily apparent, and offer both simple and advanced searching. The user should be able to limit searching by date, publication type, language, and target audience. When it is desirable, the user should be able to limit searching to peer-reviewed publications. Advanced searching should support Boolean searching and searching by exact phrase, keywords, author, title, series, ISBN, date, subjects, or classification. The interface should support saving searches and searching within search results. The user should be able to limit searches to resources that are full text and to which the user's library provides access.

Comparing interfaces to the same content involves contrasting the functionality of each and comparing the costs. For example, ERIC, a bibliographic and full-text database of education research and information sponsored by the Institute of Education Sciences of the U.S. Department of Education, is available free on the Internet. It is also available from ProQuest, EBSCOhost, and OCLC. Each version has a different interface. Some libraries consider paying more for the same e-content if they believe the interface is better or, perhaps, because they are already licensing products that use that interface. The need for one uniform user interface or a limited number of interfaces may be an important factor.

One desirable function in a user interface is an alert service. This is the ability to set up customized subject or search profiles through which users are notified when new content that matches their profiles becomes available.

Most interfaces incorporate DRM, which varies from platform to platform. One typical example is limiting the reader devices to which content can be downloaded and requiring the use of proprietary software to access the content. Many library users find this frustrating and confusing, especially when the options and limitations are not immediately obvious.

Many providers offer trials for a set period of time before the library makes a selection decision. These are an effective way to test the interface and other aspects of the product. Libraries often limit access to the trial to library staff or a small set of selected users. Opening up the trial to the entire user community can raise expectations that will not be met if the library opts not to license the product. If a trial period is not available, the library should insist on some other opportunity to explore the interface and test its functionality.

Ease of Authentication

Authentication is the process by which authorized users are verified or validated. Authorized users are defined in the license clause that describes who has permission to access and use the e-content. Authentication is the security measure used by the computer system to confirm that a user is, as nearly as can be determined, who he or she claims to be. Typical means of authentication use unique information that only the user knows or to which the user has access, such as a user name and password, personal identification number (PIN) assigned by the ILS, employee ID number, or a digital signature. Because most users have many instances of passwords, PINs, and signatures, simplifying the sign-on process has become a priority for libraries.

One simplification is to avoid the sign-on process altogether by, instead, getting the e-content provider to agree to accept any user from within a given range of IP addresses as a legitimate user. Libraries give the provider a range of IP addresses on the library's network, and the provider accepts all traffic from that range. Systems such as EZproxy (www.oclc.org/ezproxy) can extend such access outside the library's network by first authenticating users via a local user database and then allowing their remote systems to masquerade as systems on the library network.

Other authentication options attempt to simplify the situation for users by providing a single sign-on solution. This allows users to manage one user name and password that can then be the basis of their authentication on multiple provider systems. Shibboleth is a standards-based, open-source identity management system that federates identities so that a user's credentials from one security domain, such as a university, can be trusted by other organizations, such as e-content providers. Central Authentication Services (CAS, www.jasig.org/cas) and OpenAthens (www.openathens.net) are other attempts to make single sign-on viable. In the wider web community, OAuth (http://oauth.net) approaches single sign-on by allowing users to leverage accounts they already have with the likes of Google and Facebook to sign on to other services.

An important consideration when evaluating an authentication process is the ability to protect user privacy. Libraries can require a clause in licenses that prohibits content providers from collecting and using information about individual users of its products, including information about the content of a user's searches.

Regardless of the type of authentication process, it should be clear and simple and involve as few clicks to navigate as possible. Ease of authentication is an important consideration.

Accessibility

Accessibility of a resource covers several areas that fall into two broad categories: technical and design components that increase accessibility for all users, and ease of access for users with disabilities. When assessing technical and design components, the library evaluates such factors as composition and organization, navigational features, adherence to standards, and system integrity (i.e., stability and accessibility of the hosting system). Consideration should be given to how accessible the resource is to users on a technical level. What are the technical requirements of the resource in terms of browser requirements, software, hardware, service, and authentication? If users do not have the appropriate software or hardware, the resource is inaccessible. Does content offer interlinking with other resources and content by linking into and out of resources? The implementation of an OpenURL link resolver can help the user find the full text of an article and identify other pertinent resources. However, users cannot take advantage of this technology if the library does not offer OpenURL enabling.

The resource should be accessible to individuals with disabilities. Some libraries are required to comply with Section 508 of the American with Disabilities Act (ADA), which mandates that U.S. federal agencies' electronic and information technology be accessible to people with disabilities.[6] Libraries that are part of entities that receive federal funds are required to make programs and communication accessible under Section 504 of the 1973 Rehabilitation Act.[7] In May 2012, blind patrons of the Free Library of Philadelphia sued the library because it instituted an e-reader program using e-readers that are inaccessible to the print-disabled.[8] States also may have applicable laws.

Academic libraries may be able to tap a campus disability services unit to help with these issues. Public libraries may have access to a local government office or agency responsible for ADA compliance and accommodating individuals with disabilities. School systems usually have a department or individual responsible for providing reasonable appropriate accommodations for disabled youth. The interface should be accessible or the library should provide supplemental adaptive technology (e.g., text-to-speech software) or personal services to assist disabled users. Ideally, the user should be able to zoom and increase font size. Images and graphics should have alt tags or long descriptions. The ability to bypass a row of navigation links by jumping to the start of the web page content is desirable. E-books that are presented in an accessible format on an e-book reader should allow the user to choose to read the book using text-to-speech software, braille, or magnification.

Libraries may not be able to select e-resources that address all accessibility concerns, but they should consider them when making choices. At a minimum, libraries should be prepared to offer alternative solutions to meet the needs of those with access issues.

Local Service Implications and
Local Physical and Logistical Requirements

These criteria address what the library needs to provide access to and support for the resource. The library should assess the extent to which local guides and support tools must be developed, for example, a web page that offers tips and FAQ, an online tutorial, or a printed help sheet. What skill sets do library staff need to help users? To what extent should staff understand the hardware and software that the library must provide? Do in-house computers have the capacity to access and perhaps download files of the size and type offered?

Does the library's Internet connection have sufficient bandwidth capacity? Can the library provide the type of authentication the provider requires? Some resources have automatic timeouts. Although this is not necessarily a problem, the library should be able to set the parameters, such as timeout after ten minutes or thirty minutes of inactivity.

Many libraries lend e-book readers. This can help address the problem of e-content accessibility for those users who do not own these devices. A 2012 Primary Research Group report found that 39.0 percent of libraries surveyed offered e-book reading devices of some kind.[9] This service was more common with public libraries, 66.7 percent of which offered at least one e-reader; 38.5 percent of academic libraries reported offering e-book reading devices. The types of readers varied—Amazon Kindles, Sony Readers, Apple iPads, Barnes and Noble Nooks, and others. Several sources rate, compare, or recommend readers. Libraries considering acquiring e-book readers should consult the most recent resources, because options change frequently, as does their compatibility with various e-book suppliers. Not only must a library budget for acquiring these devices, it must also consider replacement costs, support, and service issues.

School libraries have some unique logistical needs. They often desire easy integration of content, including multimedia resources, with other online resources to support the curriculum and state teaching standards. The ease with which this is possible (and permission to do so) should be a decision point in selecting e-content for school libraries.

OpenURL Compliance

OpenURL provides a common linking syntax and directs users to appropriate, subscribed resources for the content they are seeking.[10] OpenURLs enable the transfer of metadata about an item (e.g., a journal article or book) from a resource where a citation is discovered (e.g., an abstracting and indexing database or the bibliography in an article or book) to a link resolver. A link resolver is an online utility that uses the OpenURL standard to link between a citation and the electronic full text of the resource cited. Typically, an OpenURL link resolver includes a knowledge base that records a library's subscriptions to e-journals and other e-resources, along with details of how to encode links to these target electronic resources. Most libraries consider OpenURL technology critical functionality and generally require OpenURL source links from resources to which they subscribe. A library considering an e-resource should ensure that it is OpenURL-compliant.

Output and Delivery Options

Libraries should understand the output and delivery options available and evaluate these in terms of local needs and expectations. Options vary across products, and some may be more applicable to e-journals or to e-books, for example. Considerations include the ability to download, print, copy to clipboard, cut and paste, and send the content as an e-mail attachment, along with any limitations (e.g., frequency, number of files, and size of file) to doing so. The ease with which these activities can be performed is also a consideration. For example, how many clicks are needed to select and attach content to an e-mail message? Can the user tag a file to allow later printing? Some products support exporting citations to various bibliographic management programs such as RefWorks, Endnote, and ProCite and generating bibliographies in the format of the user's choice. Additional options include the ability to highlight text, add bookmarks, and use annotation tools such as adding notes and comments.

Understanding restrictions enforced by DRM are important. Readers can find DRM frustrating. The web of links and instructions is often confusing, and what users perceive as onerous limitations on the ability to print and otherwise manipulate content can discourage use of these resources.

Providers frequently add output and delivery options; these should be monitored. Choosing the appropriate e-content requires understanding the output and delivery options most desired by the library and its users.

Compatibility with Mobile Devices

With an increasing volume of content accessible from and downloadable to mobile devices (smartphones, PDAs, tablet computers, e-readers), compatibility is an important criterion. Increasingly, e-content providers are offering mobile interfaces that provide most of the same features and options as the regular search interface, including access to electronic resources available from the library. The mobile interface is optimized to display web content effectively on portable devices' small screens. Libraries considering various e-content options and providers should verify that an effective mobile interface is available.

Format compatibility is an issue with digital video files, particularly end user viewing options. Different file formats require different video players, and different video players require different file players. Common video players are RealPlayer, Windows Media Player, QuickTime, Apple iTunes, and Adobe Flash. Fortunately, most video players play a variety of file types in addition to their own proprietary file formats. Most video players can be downloaded for free, but users need to be sure they have the most recent versions of the software on their computer or mobile device, and some may need more than one player to access various file types. Users frequently expect libraries to provide technical support as they seek to download and access varied digital video files. The situation for libraries is more complicated than that of users if the library wishes to provide access within the library building. Though the video player may be free, the library must ensure that current players are loaded and that they have the hardware and software to support viewing the digital video files to which they provide access.

Library e-books that are viewed online in real time via desktop and portable computers present significantly fewer compatibility issues than e-books that are downloaded onto desktop and laptop computers, e-readers, and other mobile devices. Format compatibility for the latter will remain an issue for some time. The reader marketplace changes frequently, with new models with additional capabilities offered regularly. Not all files are forward-compatible with newer devices. DRM or its absence and the software on which portable devices run determine the devices on which e-books can be read. Aggregators are working with publishers to offer compatibility with as many devices as possible and also evaluating new devices with the goal of providing flexibility to libraries and their users. Although compatibility may seem capricious, libraries are best served if they understand the issues, what their users want, and what providers offer.

Duplication or Replacement of Existing Library Resources

Uniqueness of content, capabilities, or features is an accepted criterion for selecting all types of content. This takes on added complications when selecting e-content. Many libraries initially faced this decision when deciding whether to retain print journal subscriptions, print reference resources, and indexing and abstracting tools when they began licensing the e-versions. Although users generally prefer e-versions of these materials, libraries have struggled with deciding whether to retain print as archival copies and thus duplicate the content in print and electronic formats. This issue has become less debatable as publishers have moved away from offering print versions of these resources or have made the cost of acquiring both print and electronic versions prohibitive.

Many licenses for e-books do not permit access by more than one user. To satisfy user interest in high-demand titles, such as bestsellers and recent publications, libraries may purchase access to several copies, as they have done with print books. For example, a public library might aim to have no more than three holds on a title and purchase access to sufficient copies to maintain this ratio. After the period of high demand ends, the library might reduce its subscription to a single copy.

Decisions about replacing or duplicating other types of e-content are less clear. Many library users prefer traditional formats or do not have access to the technology to access e-content outside the physical library. Some print materials, such as picture books and other books for young readers, may remain the preferred format for some time. Academic libraries are moving more rapidly than public and school libraries to replace worn or missing print books with e-books when they are available and some type of perpetual access is assured.

As is the case with all selection decisions, attention must be given to the user community being served and the mission of the specific library. Deciding the extent to which print should be retained when an e-version is available or the desirability of replacing print with an e-version is not always simple.

Availability of Data to Measure Use and Effectiveness

Libraries should examine the ability of an e-resource provider to supply data that measures use and effectiveness. These data can help assess how well an e-resource is satisfying the library's objectives and meeting the demands placed on it. Three conditions must be met to make these data available and useful. The first is identifying the desirable statistics the remote resource provider is to supply. The library community, through the International Coalition of Library Consortia (ICOLC), has taken the lead in this area. ICOLC's "Revised Guidelines for Statistical Measures of Usage of Web-Based Information Resources" define and create a common set of basic use information requirements that all electronic products should provide.[11] The statistics to be provided are

- number of sessions (logins)
- number of queries (searches)
- number of menu selections
- number of full-content units examined, downloaded, or otherwise supplied to user
- number of turn-aways, peak simultaneous users, and any other indicator relevant to the pricing model applied to the library or consortium

The second condition is that the manner in which these data are defined and counted by providers should be standardized. Project COUNTER (Counting Online Usage of Networked Electronic Resources, www.project counter.org) developed a single, integrated code of practice that normalizes how statistics are defined and counted by providers.[12] The current code of practice covers journals, databases, books, and multimedia. E-content providers who follow this code are considered COUNTER-compliant.

The final condition is that the data be provided in a consistent manner and in a way that libraries can use. Libraries have had to download data individually provider by provider and manipulate it locally or contract with a third party, such as Serials Solutions and Scholarly Stats. The National Information Standards Organization is working with interested parties in the Standardized Usage Statistics Harvesting Initiative (SUSHI).[13] SUSHI includes a versioned Web Services Description Language (WSDL) to describe the web service namespace and operation and an XML schema for COUNTER Release 4 reports. It includes a standard protocol for machine-to-machine automation of statistics harvesting that can be used by ERMs and other library systems. A few third parties are offering tools that consolidate and, in some cases, analyze COUNTER statistics.

An e-content provider should be COUNTER-compliant and able to provide the library with online access to the usage statistics. Ideally, these statistics are available in SUSHI format. At a minimum, libraries should ensure that the content provider supplies the key data points defined by ICOLC in an easily accessible manner.

DESELECTION

Deselection is the process of removing materials from a collection. In the case of e-content, this can mean identifying subscribed content for cancellation or removing e-books that have superseded content or are no longer relevant. Some e-book providers allow libraries to swap an e-book title with little or no use for another that might be used more. Libraries may decide to cancel e-content in response to subscription price increases and budgetary constraints, but other reasons apply. The product may not meet performance and content expectation; both may have changed over time. It may no longer satisfy the purpose for which it was selected. The content may be available from another provider with a better interface, more features, or lower cost. The library may have access to the content through another product. Library priorities may have changed, making investment in the product no longer

ELECTRONIC RESOURCES USE AND
IMPACT STATISTICS SUPPLEMENTING COUNTER DATA

Locally collected logins to licensed content. Using transaction
logs is one method to capture use data when the provider is not
OpenURL or COUNTER-compliant. These data do not measure
user success in locating and accessing the specific content they are
seeking, only that they logged into a resource. Users who log in
from off-site may not be counted.

Affinity strings. Affinity strings are a way to track use by categories
of users. Some academic libraries have access to data generated by
campus systems through which individuals are assigned one or
more affinity strings based on area of study or work. These might
include codes for academic unit, specific academic program, or
role (undergraduate, graduate student, faculty, etc.). A library
using these data can sort logins by, for example, academic department and status as faculty or student. Care must be taken to protect the privacy of individual users.

Link resolver use. These data can measure the number of times
users connect to a resource they locate by using an indexing or
abstracting database—that is, clicks on full-text article links.
These data depend on resources being OpenURL-compliant and
thus actionable by the link resolver. They can capture use when a
supplier is not COUNTER-compliant. Link resolver use statistics
do not track activity when a user bypasses the link resolver and
goes directly to the resource.

Thomson Reuters *Journal Citation Reports*. This bibliometric tool
provides data on impact factors for some 11,000 titles in the sciences and social sciences through citation analysis. Note, however,
that the frequency a journal is cited does not necessarily reflect its
quality.

prudent. Use may be low and no longer justify the cost. User needs may be
met more cost effectively through alternative access and delivery mechanisms, such as ILL.[14]

Deciding which of these conditions apply often requires usage data. Thus,
selecting products that provide comprehensive, comparable, and easily acces-

sible statistics is important.[15] One challenge is that usage statistics are not necessarily comparable from product to product. If, for example, a library decides to examine cost per use to determine if use justifies investment in a product, care must be taken that "use" is meaningful. Is it a measure of "full-content units examined, downloaded, or otherwise supplied to user," or a count of logins or queries, which do not necessarily reflect user success?[16] Usage statistics have little meaning if users cannot find the resource. Libraries should take care when making decisions based on these data.

Assessing user success and satisfaction with a product can be challenging. Effectiveness, impact factors, and data about outcomes can be lacking. Questions remain about how to determine which resources are of the greatest value to users and, for that matter, what makes a resource of greater or lesser value. Libraries can use focus groups to explore users' perceptions of products. Usability testing assesses the effectiveness and efficiency of an e-resource and user satisfaction with it.[17] In usability testing, representatives of the user community perform predetermined tasks while observed by researchers. Data collected are used to evaluate the degree to which the e-resource meets established criteria, including interface functionality, accessibility, compatibility with mobile devices, output options, and content that meets users' needs.

Generally, the best approach to assessing a product for retention or cancellation involves two and sometimes three different methods. Using more than one method can help eliminate biases or skewed data that can influence an evaluation.

The least problematic time to cancel a subscription to e-content is at the point of renewal. However, some licenses (e.g., Big Deals) may limit cancellations or include specific conditions, such as provider performance failure or a library's fiscal exigency, which must be met to permit cancellation. Libraries who wish to cancel during the term of the license should explore the possibility of getting a refund or credit, although this is not a common option.

SUMMARY

Selecting e-resources involves additional criteria beyond those normally considered when selecting other types of resources. These include the provider's business model; persistency of content; optimum user interface functionality; ease of authentication; accessibility that is not compromised by users' access to computing hardware, software, or the Internet, or by their physical disabilities; acceptable impact on local services and affordable local technological and logistical support; compliance with OpenURL to support linking from citation to content through a link resolver; appropriate output options matching user needs; and compatibility with mobile devices. The extent to which an e-resource under consideration duplicates or can replace existing library resources merits consideration. The availability of data to measure use and effectiveness is critical because these data can help assess the resource's value to users. Additional criteria are the availability of descriptive metadata and licensing and contractual terms, limitations, and obligations.

Making informed decisions when deselecting e-resources is as important as making informed selection decisions. Libraries assess currently licensed products to ensure that they continue to meet the expectations in place when they were selected and to compare them to new offerings on the market. E-resources should still fit within local priorities. Usage statistics, an important tool for assessing whether the cost of providing an e-resource is justified by the value it provides to users, is not without problems. Care should be taken when analyzing these data, and they should be considered in concert with qualitative measures of user success and satisfaction.

Suggested Readings

American Library Association, Digital Content and Libraries Working Group. *Digital Rights Management.* ALA DCWG Tip Sheet 1. July 2012. www.districtdispatch.org/wp-content/uploads/2012/07/drm_tip_sheet.pdf.

Apps, Ann, and Ross MacIntyre. "Why OpenURL?" *D-Lib Magazine* 12, no. 5 (May 2006). www.dlib.org/dlib/may06/apps/05apps.html.

Bleiler, Richard, and Jill Livingston. *Evaluating E-resources.* SPEC Kit 316. Washington, DC: Association for Research Libraries, 2010.

Braun, Linda W. "Now Is the Time: E-books, Teens, and Libraries." *Young Adult Library Services* 9, no. 4 (Summer 2012): 27–30.

Connaway, Lynn Silipigni, and Heather L. Wicht. "What Happened to the E-book Revolution? The Gradual Integration of E-books into Academic Libraries." *Journal of Electronic Publishing* 10, no. 3 (Fall 2007). http://quod.lib.umich.edu/j/jep/3336451.0010.302/—what-happened-to-the-e-book-revolution-the-gradual?rgn=main;view=fulltext.

Crosetto, Alice. "Weeding E-books." In *No Shelf Required 2: Uses and Management of Electronic Books,* ed. Sue Polanka, 93–101. Chicago: American Library Association, 2012.

Eggleston, Holly, and Katy Gianna. "Simplifying Licensed Resource Access through Shibboleth." *Serials Librarian* 56, no. 1/4 (2009): 209–14.

England, Lenore, and Li Fu. "Electronic Resources Evaluation Central: Using Off-the-Shelf Software, Web 2.0 Tool, and LibGuides to Manage an Electronic Resources Evaluation Process." *Journal of Electronic Resources Librarianship* 23, no. 1 (2011): 30–42.

Ferguson, Christine L. "Criteria for Selecting and Evaluating E-resources." In *Managing the Transition from Print to Electronic Journals and Resources: A Guide for Library and Information Professionals,* ed. Maria D. D. Collins and Patrick L. Carr, 29–44. New York: Routledge, 2008.

Foote, Carolyn. "Leading and Learning: Technology and E-book Adoption in School Libraries." In *No Shelf Required 2: Uses and Management of Electronic Books,* ed. Sue Polanka, 195–205. Chicago: American Library Association, 2012.

Greenwalt, R. Toby. "Developing an E-book Strategy." *Public Libraries* 51, no. 1 (Jan./Feb. 2012): 22–24.

Grogg, Jill E., and Rachel A. Fleming-May. "The Concept of Electronic Resource Usage and Libraries." *Library Technology Reports* 46, no. 6 (2010).

Hult, Patricia. "Electronic Usage Statistics." In *Electronic Resources Management in Libraries: Research and Practice,* ed. Holly Yu and Scott Breivold, 29–46. Hershey, NY: Information Science Reference, 2008.

Koehn, Shona L., and Suliman Hawamdeh. "The Acquisition and Management of Electronic Resources: Can Use Justify Cost?" *Library Quarterly* 80, no. 2 (2010): 161–74.

Magi, Trina J. "A Content Analysis of Library Vendor Privacy Policies: Do They Meet Our Standards?" *College and Research Libraries* 71, no. 3 (May 2010): 254–72.

Minčič-Obradovič, Ksenija. *E-books in Academic Libraries.* Oxford: Chandos, 2011.

Morrisey, Locke. "Data-Driven Decision Making in Electronic Collection Development." *Journal of Library Administration* 50, no. 3 (2010): 283–90.

Morrison, Andrea M., ed. *Managing Electronic Government Information in Libraries: Issues and Practices.* Chicago: American Library Association, 2008.

Mueller, Luke. "E-books in Special Libraries: Final Report of the Federal Reserve System Libraries Work Group on E-books." Oct. 14, 2010. www.governmentinfopro.com/files/fed -libraries-e-books-report—10-2010.pdf.

Myall, Carolynne, and Sue Anderson. "Can This Orthodoxy Be Saved? Enhancing the Usefulness of Collection Plans in the Digital Environment." *Collection Management* 32, no. 3/4 (2007): 235–58.

Nabe, Jonathan. "What's Next for Collection Management and Managers?" *Collection Management* 36, no. 1 (2010): 3–16.

Noh, Younghee. "A Study on Developing Evaluation Criteria for Electronic Resources in Evaluation Indicators of Libraries." *Journal of Academic Librarianship* 36, no. 1 (Jan. 2010): 41–52.

Pesch, Oliver. "Perfecting COUNTER and SUSHI to Achieve Reliable Usage Analysis." *Serials Librarian* 61, no. 3/4 (Oct./Dec. 2011): 353–65.

Petri, Ken. "Accessibility Issues in E-books and E-book Readers." In *No Shelf Required 2: Uses and Management of Electronic Books,* ed. Sue Polanka, 35–60. Chicago: American Library Association, 2012.

Porter, Michale, Matt Weaver, and Bobbi Newman. "E-book Sea Change in Public Libraries: Lending, Devices, Training, and Budgets." In *No Shelf Required 2: Uses and Management of Electronic Books,* ed. Sue Polanka, 127–44. Chicago: American Library Association, 2012.

Price, Kate, and Virginia Havergal. *E-books in Libraries: A Practical Guide.* London: Facet, 2011.

Slater, Robert. "E-books or Print Books, 'Big Deals' or Local Selections—What Gets More Use?" *Library Collections, Acquisitions, and Technical Services* 33, no. 1 (2009): 31–41.

Sprague, Nancy, and Ben Hunter. "Assessing E-books: Taking a Closer Look at E-book Statistics." *Library Collections, Acquisitions, and Technical Services* 32, no. 3/4 (2009): 150–57.

Stowers, Eva, and Cory Tucker. "Using Link Resolver Reports for Collection Management." *Serials Review* 35, no. 1 (2009): 28–34.

Sugarman, Tammy, et al., presenters. "Evaluating Usage of Non-test Resources: What the COUNTER Statistics Don't Tell You." *Serials Librarian* 60, no. 1/4 (Jan./June 2011): 83–97.

Tucker, James Cory. "Ebook Collection Analysis: Subject and Publisher Trends." *Collection Building* 31, no. 2 (2012): 40–48.

University of California Libraries. "UC Libraries Academic E-book Usage Survey." May 2011. www.cdlib.org/services/uxdesign/docs/2011/academic_ebook_usage_survey.pdf.

University of California Libraries Collections Development Committee. "The Promise of Value-Based Journal Prices and Negotiation: A UC Report and View Forward." http://libraries .universityofcalifornia.edu/cdc/valuebasedprices.pdf.

Notes

1. Peggy Johnson, *Fundamentals of Collection Development and Management*, 2nd. ed. (Chicago: American Library Association, 2009), 112–13.

2. Raphael Amit and Christoph Zott, "Value Creation in E-business," *Strategic Management Journal* 22, no. 6/7 (2001): 493–520.

3. Association of American University Presses, "Digital Book Publishing in the AAUP Community" (Spring 2011), www.aaupnet.org/images/stories/data/2011digitalsurveyreport.pdf.

4. Andres Albanese, "Citing 'Security Concerns' Penguin Pulls New Titles from OverDrive," *Publishers Weekly* (Nov. 21, 2011), www.publishersweekly.com/pw/by-topic/digital/ content-and-e-books/article/49598-citing-security-concerns-penguin-pulls-new-titles-from -overdrive-.html.

5. Michael Kelley, "Random House Reaffirms Commitment to Library Ebook Lending while Raising Prices to Wholesalers," *The Digital Shift* (Feb. 2, 2012), www.thedigitalshift .com/2012/02/ebooks/random-house-reaffirms-commitment-to-library-ebook-lending -while-raising-prices-to-wholesalers.

6. Americans with Disabilities Act of 1990, Public Law 101–336, 101st Cong. (July 26, 1990); ADA Amendments Act of 2008, Public Law 110–325, 110th Cong. (Sept. 25, 2008).

7. Rehabilitation Act of 1972, Public Law 93–112, 93rd Cong. (Sept. 26, 1973).

8. National Federation of the Blind, "National Federation of the Blind Assists in Litigation against Free Library of Philadelphia" (May 2, 2012), http://nfb.org/national-federation-blind -assists-litigation-against-philadelphia-free-library.

9. Primary Research Group, *Library Use of eBooks, 2012 Edition* (New York: Primary Research Group, 2011).

10. National Information Standards Organization, *The OpenURL Framework for Context-Sensitive Services, ANSI/NISO Z39.88–2004 (R2010)* (Baltimore: NISO, 2011).

11. International Coalition of Library Consortia, "Revised Guidelines for Statistical Measures of Usage of Web-Based Information Resources" (Oct. 4, 2006), http://icolc.net/statement/ revised-guidelines-statistical-measures-usage-web-based-information-resources.

12. Project COUNTER, "Code of Practice 4" (Apr. 2012), www.projectcounter.org/code_ practice.html. Vendors are obligated to implement Release 4 by Dec. 13, 2013 to be considered COUNTER-complaint.

13. National Information Standards Organization, "NISO Standardized Usage Statistics Harvesting Initiative (SUSHI)," www.niso.org/workrooms/sushi.

14. Cecilia Botero, Steven Carrico, and Michele Tennant, "Using Comparative Online Journal

Usage Studies to Assess the Big Deal," *Library Resources and Technical Services* 52, no. 2 (Apr. 2008): 61–68.

15. V. J. Suseela, "Application of Usage Statistics for Assessing the Use of E-journals in University of Hyderabad: A Case Study," *Electronic Library* 29, no. 6 (2011): 751–61.

16. International Coalition of Library Consortia, "Revised Guidelines."

17. Jody Condit Fagen, "Usability Testing of a Large, Multidisciplinary Library Database: Basic Search and Visual Search," *Information Technology and Libraries* 25, no. 3 (Sept. 2006): 140–50; Alexei Oulanov, "Business Administration Students' Perceptions of Usability of the Business Source Premier Database: A Case Study," *Electronic Library* 26, no. 4 (2008): 505–19.

CHAPTER 3

SELECTION AND ORDER PLACEMENT

SOME TEN YEARS AGO, Gorman observed that library collections comprise locally owned physical materials, physical materials owned elsewhere but available through ILL, e-content that the library owns or to which it subscribes, and "free" electronic materials.[1] These hybrid collections require rebalancing libraries' staffing and financial resources. Traditional approaches to collection development policies, practices, and responsibilities, and acquisition workflow have required reconsideration. This chapter addresses e-content selection and order placement activities. It builds on the previous chapter, which explores criteria for selecting and evaluating e-content.

SELECTION

Deciding the e-content to add to a collection either through purchase or subscription (lease) requires identifying the content desired; evaluating providers, their services, and the quality of the product; seeking the best price; analyzing the license agreement, and determining the most sustainable option. The same steps apply to decisions about free e-content, realizing that content that is freely available does involve costs to the library. These decisions should be made in the context of the library's collection policies, especially the sections or supplemental policies that address e-content. Thus selection should involve comparing selection candidates against the library's established selection criteria. A key decision point is whether the library can afford to provide access to a given e-resource initially and in the longer term. Even free e-resources require expenditure of staff time for identification, selection, evaluation, cataloging, link maintenance, and training.

Some types of selection decisions may be guided by collection development policies. Typical areas addressed are migrating to e-only for journals and other continuing resources, e-preferred for books, and guidelines for selecting free web-based content. Libraries increasingly have policies that determine when cancelling a print subscription in favor of the e-version is appropriate. Some have extended this policy to cover other types of resources. Others may address this preference in their approval plans, with the e-version of a book to be provided if both print and electronic are available.

MIGRATING TO ELECTRONIC-ONLY FORMAT

Many libraries have decided to cancel print subscriptions to journals, indexes and abstracts, and other reference sources when migrating to the e-version. Normally, this decision, often called "electronic preferred," is guided by a policy that specifies when this is appropriate. The most common requirements are that the product license guarantees perpetual and post-cancellation access to subscribed content. There are possible exceptions, such as these:

- The print version is heavily used.
- Significant differences exist between the print and electronic versions, with the e-version offering additional content.
- The print version has significant artifactual or aesthetic value.
- Images and graphics in the print versions are demonstrably better.
- Online access is based on a continued print subscription.
- The license does not permit using the e-version for ILL.
- The library has a consortial commitment to retain the print format.
- The e-version is provided by an aggregator that cannot guarantee continued access.

If the library acquires e-backfiles, a second decision addresses retention of print backfiles. Withdrawing extensive runs of print journals, indexes and abstracts, and other reference sources is attractive because they require considerable shelf space and are often little or never used. Generally, the same criteria above apply. In lieu of withdrawal, libraries may decide to move these backfiles to off-site storage.

Librarians usually select free e-content title by title as they learn about specific free resources. These may be websites, e-journals, e-books, audio, and multimedia. Some libraries have developed policies governing the conditions under which resources freely available on the Internet are cataloged locally through the creation of a record and link in the local catalog. A common overarching principle is that the same criteria used for selection, acquisition, and cataloging other resources should apply to free e-content. Some categories of free e-content, such as free e-journals that continue existing cataloged print or electronic titles and new open-access scholarly journals, may be approved without additional review. Some may be considered selectively if they are deemed stable, of particular local value, and not adequately indexed elsewhere. Categories of resources that are excluded might include commercial websites and association websites. The e-content on these websites is often updated, replaced, and removed, and the links are often unstable. Libraries are less consistent in their policies about cataloging public domain publications hosted by the Library of Congress Digital Collections (www.loc.gov/library/libarch-digital.html), Google Books (http://books.google .com), HathiTrust Digital Library (http://catalog.hathitrust.org), Internet Archives E-books and Texts (http://archive.org/details/texts), Project Gutenberg (www .gutenberg.org), and others. Many libraries selectively catalog these e-books; others do not because they are readily discoverable through the hosting site and often a simple browser search.

Federal and some state and local government documents present a special case. By 2009, approximately 97 percent of new U.S. federal government documents were freely available digitally, and approximately three-quarters of new documents existed exclusively in digital form.[2] These are, for the most part, easily discoverable via government websites and title and keyword searching using browsers. Libraries that do not participate in the federal depository program need to decide if records for these documents should be added to the local catalog. Many older print government materials have been or will be digitized by libraries, vendors, and mass digitization programs, enhancing the accessibility of these materials. Generally, U.S. federal documents are in the public domain and available full-text online if digitized by libraries or as part of a mass digitization project. If, however, a commercial vendor has done the digitization, libraries must pay to access the content.

Some librarians diligently search for free e-content that they think meets local needs and priorities. Libraries should be judicious when selecting these resources. Adding descriptive information about these resources to the catalog or a subject-based library website requires staff time. Links go bad and need to be rechecked, another drain on staff. Many users can locate these resources on their own using the same search strategies that librarians would use. Each library should decide if the staff time and effort needed to locate, describe, and link to these resources is justified.

CASE STUDY:

LOCATING APPROPRIATE FREE DIGITAL CONTENT

A library in Michigan is interested in assembling a collection of free digital content to meet the needs of people interested in Michigan's involvement with the Civil War. The following search strategies and results are examples of approaches to identifying e-content of value to this library.

- Search Google Books and discover *Record of Service of Michigan Volunteers in the Civil War 1861–1865,* by George H. Turner (Kalamazoo, MI: Ihling Bros. and Everard, 1871). This is a free book available full-text through Google Books, retrieved by searching "Michigan Civil War" and limiting the results to free Google books.
- Search Project Gutenberg and discover *Personal Recollections of a Cavalryman with Custer's Michigan Cavalry Brigade in the Civil War,* by James Harvey Kidd (Ionia, MI: Sentinel Press, 1908). This free book is available through Project Gutenberg and was retrieved with the search "Michigan Civil War."
- Search Google by entering "Michigan Civil War" and discover the Michigan Government Television site "'Oh, Could They But Speak!' The History and Importance of Michigan's Civil War Battle Flags," which is a package of curriculum materials that includes a link to a 2003 documentary video with the same title available online. The same search results include "The Michigan Experience: The American Civil War Years," produced by iMichigan Productions, which includes a four-part television series and "an open source free online E-Learning Center for students, teacher, and life-long learners."

Warning: Neither creating a library website with these and similar links nor cataloging these resources in the local catalog is necessarily recommended. The processes of locating appropriate free content, describing it, and ensuring that links remain viable are time-consuming tasks. Making such content available might be justified to provide supplemental resources for a course, library exhibit, speaker, or another community event—and then removed when activity concludes.

E-resource Selection and Management Responsibility

The assignment of selection responsibilities for e-content varies with types and sizes of libraries and the total cost of the e-product. This, too, may be clarified in collection policies. In larger libraries, responsibility for selecting individual titles and subject-based collections may be assigned to individual library selectors, liaisons, or subject specialists, to a senior collections officer, or a selection committee. The senior collections officer may be the final decision maker even in those cases where the product is selected by an individual librarian or a committee. Larger collections of content or those with high cost are generally selected by a senior collections officer or a senior library administrator and often within the context of choices made by consortia of which the library is a member. In smaller libraries with fewer staff and smaller budgets, selection responsibility for all e-content is likely held by one person. In school libraries and media centers, selection may be handled centrally at the district level and also involve input from teachers. Librarians in individual school libraries may have authority to select resources that meet local school needs; for example, a Spanish immersion school might select e-content targeted at this curriculum.

Selection can be at the micro level (title by title) or the macro level. Title-by-title e-book selection is facilitated when the library's book vendor includes e-books in its online selection tools. In macro selection, access is acquired to packages of titles from a single publisher or an aggregator offering bundled subject-based or age-appropriate collections from a variety of publishers. An increasingly larger amount of e-content is added to libraries by macro selection.

Libraries that use approval plans usually can include e-books in the plan, another form of macro selection. Librarians have selection responsibility to the extent that they design the profile, specifying the criteria for titles that will be supplied automatically or that will appear on periodic notification lists from the approval plan vendor. In the latter case, the selector chooses individual titles from lists generated by the approval plan vendor that match predefined profiles. When including e-books in an approval plan, the library should determine the e-book publishers with which the approval plan vendor works and ensure that a significant number of frontlist e-books are available at the time of publication.

Libraries are involving users in selection of individual e-titles through patron-driven acquisition, also called patron-initiated purchasing, demand-driven acquisition, or books-on-demand. In this model, the decision to purchase a title is driven by users accessing the item's bibliographic record in the local online public access catalog a specified number of times or for a specified length of time. This approach, most commonly found in academic libraries, is also used in other types of libraries including schools.[3] Librarians have some degree of control by setting parameters around the titles that are loaded into the catalog and thus eligible for patron selection and by identifying the users who are eligible to initiate such acquisition. Limitations begin by specifying the types of records loaded in the catalog and may involve reader level, maximum price above which librarian review is needed, currency (imprint data), language, exclusions (e.g., textbooks, popular fiction, repair manuals, publishers), and triggers needed to generate a purchase. Triggers vary among providers. Common triggers are a set number of continuous minutes of viewing, set number of unique page views by a single user, set number of "loans," printing of any pages, or a combination of these. Tables of contents and index pages are often not counted. Another decision is when (or if) unused and thus unselected titles are removed from the catalog.

Patron-driven acquisition is not universally accepted as an effective selection option.[4] Proponents see it as an extension of a common practice in libraries to purchase books requested via ILL and a way to acquire materials missed in the usual selection processes. The method is valued because it builds a collection that quickly and directly meets users' needs. However, problems can arise even when parameters are set by librarians. Some users, particularly undergraduates, can be voracious and often undiscriminating in their selections. A single patron at the University of Mississippi selected nearly 170 books in one year, equal to one quarter of total patron-driven acquisitions in that period.[5] Limiting the categories of approved users to, for example, graduate students, faculty, and researchers in an academic library or teachers in a school library is one way to reduce indiscriminate purchasing. Also, budgeting for patron-driven acquisition can be complicated. Early implementers of the method often found that funds allocated to it were expended long before the budget year ended. The most frequent library concern is the extent to which the library is abdicating its role in building collections that both satisfy current users and meet needs of future users.

Larger academic, research, and public libraries and large school districts frequently have one or more electronic resources librarians. These individuals, though not necessarily having selection responsibilities, are responsible for negotiating, managing, and interpreting licenses for all types of e-content. They also may have one or more of the following duties associated with the life cycle of e-resources: establishing resource trials, troubleshooting access problems and providing other types of technical support, working with vendors, resolving OpenURL technical issues, managing an ERM system, maintaining accurate holdings data in the library's knowledge base, resolving license violations, and obtaining, compiling, and analyzing usage data. Often the electronic resources librarian represents the library in consortial e-content decision making. In some libraries, the electronic resources librarian has responsibilities for e-resource acquisition, renewal, cancellation, or cataloging.

ACQUISITION

Once a librarian has selected an item, a supplier must be identified and the item ordered. In libraries, this process continues to be called acquisition and is often performed by acquisitions or serials staff even if nothing physical is acquired and ownership does not transfer to the library. Here, also, the lines of responsibility are blurring because of the continuing nature of many orders for e-content. The process of activating or placing an order varies considerably and depends on the procedures and workflow in each library. In some libraries the steps the librarian follows for initiating an order for e-content parallel those used for other types of content. In other libraries the process is quite different. Many libraries use online order forms that are delivered to the acquisitions staff; others may accept order requests via e-mail or in paper. At a minimum, the selecting librarian provides author, title, publisher, imprint date, ISBN or ISSN, cost, budget or fund number to be billed, the location to which the item will go (if applicable), if the item is an added copy, and his or her name. If the library has an account with a book vendor offering online ordering, the librarian may place the order directly with the vendor or queue it for subsequent review and activation by acquisitions staff. If the item to be ordered is a serial or other continuing resource, the librarian indicates the starting date or volume and whether backfiles should be purchased.

Additional information is required for e-content. Orders are normally not placed until the license is negotiated and a contract signed. Some libraries may have a separate process for ordering each type of e-content; others may use the same process for all e-resources. The latter is often a practical approach because the ordering distinctions between e-book, e-serials and other continuing e-resources, and other types of e-content are blurring. For example, e-books may be sold with multiyear access fees, which require a continuing commitment from the collections budget and extended tracking by acquisitions staff, whereas e-journals backfiles may require a firm order.

In addition to the information listed above, selectors are likely asked to provide

- URL, if available
- if the order is for a package of titles
- if all titles or only selected titles in the package are desired (if a package)
- contact information if the selector has been working with a sales representative
- type of resource (e.g., book, index, journal reference sources, streaming media)
- if the subscription to print should be continued (if an existing print subscription is active)
- if the request is for a trial (with start and end date), one-time or backfile purchase, subscription, or standing order
- any special information about cost and pricing, including such information as "free with print" or special discounts
- if a license with the content provider is already in place

Supplemental information might include whether MARC records are available with an e-book package, if additional software and hardware are needed, and the number of simultaneous users if the license does not allow unlimited access. Submitting an order for e-content may serve as a trigger to involve the electronic resources librarian, if the library has one, in license review and negotiation.

In smaller libraries, selecting and ordering e-resources may reside with the same person. If this is the case, the information given above remains necessary to move forward with order placement.

E-CONTENT SOURCES

Even with appropriate and verified information in hand, placing orders for e-content can be bewildering, especially for e-books. Confusion arises from the variety and number of business models, access options available, and the number and different types of suppliers and the formats and content they provide. Frequently, libraries have made comprehensive decisions guiding these choices early in their move into developing digital collections, opting, for example, to use a specific subscription agent for e-journals and a specific aggregator for e-books. In some instances, the choices made by selectors drive the decision about the content provider with which the order is to be placed. For example, a selector may want to ensure that e-books can be downloaded to as many types of reader devices as possible or that the provider offers pay-per-view.

Content can be leased, purchased, or pay-per-view. Leased content is often referred to as the subscription model because the library pays an annual subscription fee to access the content. This approach differs from subscriptions for print content, which give the library ownership of the content acquired during the term of the subscription. Subscriptions to e-content typically do not ensure perpetual access at the end of the subscription period, unless this is negotiated in the license. The library also may pay an annual platform or access fee. Fees may be waived if a negotiated purchase amount is spent with the provider annually. Some providers calculate annual fees based on existing collection use data. With purchased or owned content, the library pays a one-time fee and has access in perpetuity, with a license agreement articulating the terms of use and archival access. Some providers offer multiple options (lease, purchase, pay-per-view).

Patron-driven acquisition generally means that the library purchases the titles selected by users and thus owns them. This approach may be used for books, audiobooks, and media. The library also may pay an annual access fee if the content resides on the provider's site and is not downloaded by the library and managed locally, which can be costly and labor-intensive.

A variety of access models are possible. These include unlimited simultaneous users, limited simultaneous users (e.g., three simultaneous users with others turned away), single user, and pay-per-view with either the library or the user paying. The access model is defined in the license.

Another decision area is the type of content delivered. Depending on the provider, content may be available as page images, PDF, HTML, EPUB, Windows Media Audio, MP3, MPEG, or other proprietary formats. E-content may be accessed online or may be downloadable in full or part and, through DRM, the devices to which files can be downloaded may be limited.

Comparing options can be time-consuming. Acquisitions staff work with publishers, vendors who specialize in electronic content, and their existing suppliers, who also offer e-products in addition to their usual products and services, to explore possible suppliers, identify pricing options, and compare licenses and terms of availability.

E-BOOKS

E-books may be ordered directly from publishers, aggregators, or vendors. Some publishers do not allow vendors or aggregators to handle their titles and make their publications available only through their own online platforms. Not all publishers make e-books available to libraries.

Practces of the "big six" publishers (Random House, Penguin, Harper-Collins, Simon and Schuster, Hachette, and Macmillan) vary significantly. Random House allows unrestricted access to all of its e-books in libraries, although it raised e-book prices for popular titles significantly in early 2012.[6] In late 2011, Penguin announced that it would no longer make new e-books or new digital audiobooks available to libraries but reversed this stance in April 2013. Hachette sells only older e-books to libraries but increased prices for these older materials by an average of 220 percent in late 2012. Harper Collins limits e-books to twenty-six circulations and then the library has to buy a new copy. As of this writing, Simon and Schuster, Hachette, and Macmillan do not make e-books available to libraries at all. One assumes that publishers are concerned that people will not buy the books in print or e-book format if they can borrow them from libraries, yet a *Library Journal* survey on libraries and e-book usage reported that more than 50 percent of library users purchase books by an author to which they were introduced in the library.[7] Some publishers that do not make e-books available to libraries do offer their digital audiobooks to libraries. The e-book area is dynamic and changes rapidly. Monitoring the market, surveying publishers' distribution mechanisms, and consulting with vendors and aggregators should be regular practices.

Libraries may have more room for price negotiation when buying directly from publishers because no intermediary is involved, although not all publishers are willing to negotiate. Libraries that work directly with publishers may need to negotiate business models and license agreements multiple times. Public libraries are less likely than other types of libraries to acquire e-books directly from publishers. A Primary Research Group 2012 study found that only 0.5 percent of e-book orders placed by public libraries went directly to publishers.[8] Corporate and legal libraries are more likely to order e-books from publishers, especially those publishers whose materials are targeted to those libraries' collecting area. Academic libraries are less likely to order individual titles from publishers; when they do acquire e-books directly from publishers, they are most often packages of titles, usually scoped by topic and year of publication. One advantage of working with publishers that offer book, journal, or multimedia content (or all three) is that the publisher may provide access to all its formats through a single interface. This may be a modest benefit because libraries usually work with several providers, each with its own interface for e-content, requiring users to learn multiple interfaces.

Some libraries have purchased reading devices that they lend to users.[9] Often the library preloads content onto the device. The library may acquire content from an online e-content seller such as Amazon or Barnes and Noble. Libraries loan the content under the doctrine of first sale (section 109 of the U.S. Copyright Act), which permits libraries to lend materials once ownership has been transferred to the library. However, one well-known book dealer has the following statement on its website: "Upon your download of digital content and payment of any applicable fees (including applicable taxes), the content provider grants you a non-exclusive right to view, use, and display such digital content . . . and solely for your personal, non-commercial use. Digital Content is licensed, not sold, to you by the content provider." Pike addressed the challenges that e-content has created for the doctrine of first sale:

> Two important limitations in the doctrine have restricted its applicability to most forms of digital content. The first is the requirement of "lawful ownership." Most software, databases, and other digital content is licensed, which limits the level of "ownership" that the user obtains. And second, the doctrine applies to a particular "copy" of a work. Digital distribution doesn't transfer the particular copy of a work, but it makes a new, identical copy that is distributed.[10]

The extent to which the doctrine of first sale applies to e-content downloaded to devices that are loaned to patrons is a gray area not yet tested in court.

School libraries and media centers are often interested in providing multiple copies of the same book on e-readers for group use.[11] Group pricing for consortial access and simultaneous users remains a challenge. Some schools have sought to use reader devices that are preloaded and loaned to students. However, the individual consumer-focused business model of such sellers as Amazon (Kindle) and Barnes and Noble (Nook) does not work well when schools want to purchase multiple copies of a title for use by a class or reading group. School libraries and media centers continue to seek viable solutions to meet this need.

Aggregators

Aggregators gather titles from several publishers and present them on a single platform. Some aggregators give the library the option of customizing the interface that affiliated users see. Titles typically can be licensed on either a subscription or purchase model and are available in subject packages or on a title-by-title basis. The delivery platforms vary from aggregator to aggregator, as do their features and functions. Each aggregator has a unique pricing model. Some charge annual fees depending on the collection to which the library subscribes. Some bundled collections are purchased with one-time fees.

A library working with an aggregator often can negotiate a single license agreement and select one business model, providing access to hundreds of publishers and thousands of titles on one interface. Nearly 61 percent of libraries surveyed by Primary Research Group in 2011 used aggregators.[12] However, aggregators sell only the titles that publishers make available to them. Publishers may not offer backlist titles or top sellers to aggregators and may embargo new content or withdraw content from the aggregator as agreements change. Libraries may have limited opportunity to negotiate prices because aggregators' revenue is shared with publishers. Because aggregators represent hundreds of publishers, they must renegotiate changes in business models, DRM, or license terms with all the publishers whose content they offer.

Many libraries work with more than one e-book aggregator because aggregators have different business models and platforms and handle books from different publishers. Comparing two or more aggregators' options, assessing patron satisfaction, and monitoring technological development can inform decisions about the most appropriate suppliers to use.

Some aggregators shape their services and collections to a particular type of library or offer different services and collections targeted to different library types. Most aggregators offer a variety of options and access models from which libraries can choose. A list of offerings might consist of

- title-by-title selection (i.e., firm orders)
- pay-per-view, sometimes called short-term loan or pay-per-use, through which the user may access the book for a set period (e.g., one day, one week, one month) for a fee
- purchase with perpetual access
- patron-driven acquisition
- subscription (i.e., leasing access for the term of the license)
- subject-based packages or packages targeted to specific user groups for purchase or lease
- unlimited simultaneous access
- ability to read online and download e-books to desktop and laptop computers and reader devices
- ability to use chapters for course reserves

Several aggregators integrate their offering with vendors. In this model, the library works with the vendor to acquire titles handled by the aggregator.

Vendors

Vendors, sometimes called jobbers or wholesalers, are suppliers or providers of goods and services through which libraries obtain resources instead of dealing directly with a publisher. Vendors are similar to e-content aggregators in that they consolidate ordering and billing and often negotiate licenses, but they differ in that most do not have an e-book interface. Libraries usually work with one vendor or a limited number to gain efficiencies and take advantage of discounted prices and consolidated invoicing. In addition, the greater the expenditure with a vendor, the lower the service fee. Vendors often can offer materials from publishers that do not deal directly with libraries, but, like aggregators, vendors can sell only content that publishers make available.

Most vendors offer full processing including cataloging services; electronic transfer of ordering, billing, and bibliographic data; and discounts on most of the items they handle, although e-books may not be discounted. As noted above, vendors often partner with one or more e-book aggregators. An advantage of working with a vendor is the ability to integrate e-book selection, record loading, invoicing, and processing with that in place for print resources. A typical list of offerings from a vendor might be

- title-by-title selection
- integrated digital and print approval plans and digital notification plans with the option of setting "e-preferred"
- patron-driven acquisition, often based on profiles developed by the library
- pay-per-view with option to purchase after set number of views
- packages of titles developed by aggregators
- packages of titles either created by the vendor or assembled according to a library's specifications
- duplication control through linking of digital and print versions of titles
- web-based acquisition and collection development tools for searching, selecting, and ordering
- electronic data interchange for orders and invoicing with library management systems
- digital cataloging records
- preprogrammed and customized reports

As traditional vendors have increased their offering of e-books from both publishers and aggregators, more libraries are using them to provide these materials. Libraries in a Primary Research Group sample placed 41.8 percent of total e-book orders through e-book divisions of traditional book vendors and distributors in 2011.[13]

Choosing where to place a book order is not as simple as deciding if a publisher, aggregator, or book vendor is the appropriate supplier. Many book vendors serve as intermediaries for one or more e-content aggregators. Because access to e-books is often subscription-based, many journal subscription agents also offer e-book and audiobook ordering (usually as packages) via their management platforms. Subscription agents also may handle aggregator collections. By using a vendor or subscription agent with which it already has a relationship, a library can leverage existing services without establishing a new account with an aggregator.

E-JOURNALS AND OTHER CONTINUING RESOURCES

E-journals may be ordered title by title directly from the publisher, or a subscription agent may be used. E-journal publishers offer the ability to order title by title or to order packages of titles (often a publisher's complete title list) covered by a multiyear agreement (the "Big Deal"). During the past few years, some academic and research libraries in the United States, Canada, and United Kingdom have abandoned Big Deal subscriptions, opting to subscribe only to their highest use journals. Despite this retreat from the Big Deal, the 2012 edition of the *Survey of Scholarly Journal Licensing and Acquisition Practices* reported that U.S. academic and research libraries acquired 41.7 percent of their journals in bundles of fifty or more titles.[14] Publishers often offer the most cost-effective support for large, subscription-based packages. Frequently libraries work through consortia when acquiring access to publisher journal packages. Some serial titles can be ordered only from the publisher, although this is more common for society journals.

Subscription agents serve as intermediaries between libraries and publishers. Libraries place orders and prepay subscriptions through their agent, who then places orders with and pays publishers, who then supply content to libraries. Subscription agents often can support single-subscription electronic purchases more cheaply than a library can on its own. They offer many value-added services that help libraries manage subscriptions to journals and standing orders. These are covered by the service fee the serials agent charges. When a library uses a subscription agent that is already handling its print journals, ordering, invoicing, claiming, renewals, reports, and other services associate with e-journals are integrated with those in place for print subscriptions.

A typical list of services offered by a subscription agent might include

- title searching
- title-by-title ordering
- title lists
- e-package ordering and management
- claims and renewals processing
- e-journal registration and access support
- licensing assistance
- notification of title changes, mergers, and cessations
- price projections
- web-based management system for placing and tracking orders
- consolidated invoices
- electronic data interchange for orders and invoicing with library management systems
- preprogrammed and customized reports
- consolidated COUNTER usage statistics

Some subscription agents and other types of vendors offer services and products that help libraries adapt to new economic and technological circumstances. This has been described as the transition from subscription agent to information solution provider.[15] For example, several are expanding and integrating their operations to offer ERM systems, knowledge bases, support for A–Z lists, and more.

Indexing and abstracting resources are a form of continuing resource and, as such, are usually available through subscription agents, although some may be available only from their publishers. These resources, often called databases, may be available from different suppliers, each of which packages the content differently with different interfaces. Libraries are advised to set up trials to compare content and interfaces.

Two important sources for e-journals and e-books are JSTOR and Project Muse. Both are similar to aggregators in that they pull together titles from several publishers and provide access through a single interface. JSTOR (www .jstor.org), a not-for-profit organization, offers licensed access to digitized backfiles of more than 1,400 scholarly journals. Access to most titles is controlled by a delay set by the publisher, called a moving wall, that determines the period between which the current journal volume is issued and the latest volume is available through JSTOR. This normally ranges from one to five years. In addition, the JSTOR Current Scholarship Program provides access to both current titles and their backfiles, beginning when the titles became digital or, for titles not online, one year ahead of the moving wall. Libraries can select subject-based packages of journal titles and several primary source collections. JSTOR serves public libraries and libraries in higher education, secondary schools, government, nonprofit institutions, and museums. In addition, JSTOR began offering e-books in June 2012, partnering with several scholarly publishers and university presses.

Project MUSE (http://muse.jhu.edu), also a not-for-profit organization, provides access to peer-reviewed digital humanities and social sciences journals and, since early 2012, e-books. Libraries can choose from interdisciplinary journal collections and two broad collections in the humanities or social sciences. Project MUSE is the sole source of some journals from university presses and scholarly societies. It offers current subscriptions and also backfiles for several titles. The e-book collection is made available in partnership with the University Press e-book Consortium. The books are full text, in PDF, and retrievable at the chapter level. Because the e-books have no DRM attached, users at libraries that have purchased them can print, copy, download, and save content. Books are available in packaged collections by date or subject for purchase or through access-only subscriptions.

MEDIA

New library audio streaming and download services from content vendors continue to emerge. Media (audio and video) may be accessed online (streaming in real time) or downloaded from a remote server to a computer or other device, depending on the manner in which the provider offers it and choices made by the library. Streaming is a method of delivering audio and video signals to computers over the Internet. Instead of downloading a file before being able to listen to or view it, the user hears the sound and views the video as the data arrives at the computer. The data are buffered for a few seconds before playback begins. As the audio or video plays, more data are arriving (or streaming) and, as long as the data are streaming, the content continues to play. Streaming video may be called video-on-demand, or VOD.

When e-content is downloaded by a user, it normally is treated as a circulation transaction. Libraries have the ability to set the length of time an item can be used by (i.e., checked out to) a patron. When the end of the loan period is reached, the patron may have the option to renew the loan, or the content simply may disappear from the patron's computer or other device.

Access models for media parallel those for other types of e-content. Placing the order requires selecting options—unlimited simultaneous users, limited simultaneous users, single user, pay-per-view.

Some e-content aggregators offer videos and music as well as books and audiobooks for download. Often, the user must download free proprietary software from the content provider to download content. In some cases, a free mobile app is needed to transfer content that was first downloaded to a computer onto a mobile device. Aggregators provide links on their website to the necessary software.

Several aggregators or distributors specialize in educational audio and video e-content. Most streaming video available to libraries and schools consists of educational content and documentaries. Media distributors, similar to e-book distributors, are subject to the arrangements made with the creators and other owners of the intellectual property. For this reason, leasing music and video is a more common option than purchasing. However, some suppliers have purchased the rights to content (or acquired the original owner rights) and made it available for purchase, thereby ensuring the library's perpetual access.

PLACING THE ORDER

Libraries usually continue to call the order for e-content a purchase order although the content may be leased and not technically purchased. Purchase orders are generated when initiating a firm order, standing order, subscription, or lease to access content. In addition to the information provided by the selector, orders for e-resources usually require providing the supplier with

- institutional IP addresses, including proxy servers
- technical contact name, address, phone and fax numbers, e-mail address
- licensing contact name, address, phone and fax numbers, e-mail address
- start date
- number of simultaneous users (if applicable)
- bill-to address

Placing an order with a supplier of print books, print journals, DVDs, and CDs initiates the purchase, and the item is shipped to the library. Placing an order for e-content seldom leads to opening access to the resource. As Bosch, Promis, and Sugnet note, "The purchase order is a formality; the signing of the license is considered the point of purchase."[16]

SUMMARY

Selecting e-content begins with establishing criteria for selecting e-resources and developing policies that guide their application and associated decisions. Responsibilities for selection may be assigned to individual librarians, committees, library administrators, or a combination of these. Patron-driven-acquisition approaches give library users a role in selection. E-content may be selected title by title, in packages, or through approval plans. A key position in many libraries is the electronic resources librarian, who may or may not select materials but usually has responsibilities for other steps in e-content management, particularly licensing. The lines of responsibility for placing orders are blurring and may be assigned to the individual who selects the item or to staff in either an acquisitions or serials unit. The selector provides details about the item that facilitate placing an order.

Determining the appropriate e-content supplier can be challenging and requires decisions in many areas, including whether to purchase, lease, or use a pay-per-view model; the access model; and the format in which content is delivered. Most e-content is ordered from publishers, aggregators, subscription agents, or vendors. Some offer e-content targeted to particular markets or focus on a specific medium (e.g., video). Many suppliers offer e-books and audio e-books, e-journals and other continuing resources, and media—and a suite of services designed to meet the needs of libraries. Libraries can leverage a supplier's services by consolidating orders with a limited number of suppliers and simplify the user experience by limiting the number of interfaces that need to be learned.

Once the specific e-content and the appropriate supplier are selected, the order is ready to be placed. Placing an order does not, however, automatically implement access. Nearly all e-content, regardless of how delivered and accessed, requires a signed license.

Suggested Readings

Bergstrom, Ted. C. "Librarians and the Terrible Fix: Economics of the Big Deal." July 2010.
    http://works.bepress.com/ted_bergstrom/111.

Bosch, Stephen, et al. "Do Libraries Still Need Book Vendors and Subscription Agents?" Oct. 2011. www.ala.org/ala/mgrps/divs/alcts/resources/z687/vend.cfm.

Buczyniski, James A. "The Library Patron Prefers Listening: Living in Ray Bradbury's Personal Audio Universe." *Internet Reference Services Quarterly* 11, no. 2 (2006): 97–103.

Grigson, Anna. "An Introduction to E-book Business Models and Suppliers." In *E-books in Libraries: A Practical Guide,* ed. Kate Price and Virginia Havergal, 21–36. London: Facet, 2011.

Hinken, Susan, and Emily J. McElroy. "Consortial Purchasing of E-books: Orbis Cascade Alliance." In *The No Shelf Required Guide to E-book Purchasing,* ed. Sue Polanka, 8–13. Chicago: American Library Association, 2011.

Hodges, Dracine, Cyndi Preston, and Marsha J. Hamilton. "Patron-Initiated Collection Development: Progress of a Paradigm Shift." *Collection Management* 35, no. 3/4 (2010): 208–21.

Laskowski, Mary S. *Guide to Video Acquisitions in Libraries: Issues and Best Practices.* ALCTS Acquisitions Guide 15. Chicago: American Library Association, 2011.

Martin, Jim, and Raik Zaghloul. "Planning for the Acquisition of Information Resources Management Core Competencies." *New Library World* 112, no. 7/8 (2011): 313–20.

Morris, Carolyn, and Lisa Sibert. "Acquiring E-books." In *No Shelf Required: E-books in Libraries,* ed. Sue Polanka, 95–124. Chicago: American Library Association, 2011.

Nixon, Judith M., Robert S. Freeman, and Suzanne M. Ward, eds. "Patron-Driven Acquisitions: An Introduction and Literature Review." *Collection Management* 35, no. 3/4 (2010).

Polanka, Sue. "Purchasing E-books in Libraries: A Maze of Opportunities and Challenges." In *The No Shelf Required Guide to E-book Purchasing,* ed. Sue Polanka, 4–7. Chicago: American Library Association, 2011.

Pomerantz, Sarah. B. "The Role of the Acquisitions Librarian in Electronic Resources Managements." *Journal of Electronic Resources Librarianship* 22, no. 1/2 (2010): 40–48.

Price, Kate. "E-books for Free: Finding, Creating, and Managing Freely Available Texts." In *E-books in Libraries: A Practical Guide,* ed. Kate Price and Virginia Havergal, 53–70. London: Facet, 2011.

Rupp-Serrano, Karen, Sarah Robbins, and Danielle Cain. "Canceling Print Serials in Favor of Electronic: Criteria for Decision Making." *Library Collections, Acquisitions, and Technical Services* 26, no. 4 (Winter 2002): 369–78.

Shen, Lisa, et al. "Head First into the Patron-Driven Acquisition Pool: A Comparison of Librarian Selections versus Patron Purchases." *Journal of Electronic Resources Librarianship* 23, no. 3 (2011): 203–18.

Slater, Robert. "Why Aren't E-books Gaining More Ground in Academic Libraries? E-book Use and Perceptions: A Review of Published Literature and Research." *Journal of Web Librarianship* 4, no. 4 (2010): 305–31.

Turner, Rollo. "The Vital Link: The Role of the Intermediary in E-resources" (posted March 31, 2006). In *The E-resources Management Handbook,* ed. Graham Stone. http://uksg.metapress .com/content/eac8e0trmv23g78r/fulltext.pdf. *The E-resources Management Handbook* is an open-access publication on e-resource management, published by the UKSG. Chapters continue to be added.

Ward, Suzanne M. *Guide to Implementing and Managing Patron-Driven Acquisitions.* ALCTS Acquisitions Guides Series 16. Chicago: Association for Library Collections and Technical Services, American Library Association, 2012.

Weicher, Maureen, and Tian Xiao Zhang. "Unbundling the 'Big Deal.' with Pay-per-View of E-journal Articles." *Serials Librarian* 63, no. 1 (2012): 28–37.

Zhang, Tian Xiao. "Pay-per-View: A Promising Model of E-articles Subscription for Middle/Small Sized Academic Libraries in the Digital Age." *Libraries in the Digital Age (LIDA) Proceedings* 12, (2012). http://ozk.unizd.hr/proceedings/index.php/lida2012/article/view/8.

Notes

1. Michael Gorman, "Collection Development in Interesting Times: A Summary," *Library Collections, Acquisitions, and Technical Services* 24, no. 4 (Winter 2003): 459–62.

2. Roger C. Schonfeld and Ross Housewright, *Documents for a Digital Democracy: A Model for the Federal Depository Library Program in the 21st Century* (New York: Ithaka S+R, 2009), www.arl.org/bm~doc/documents-for-a-digital-democracy.pdf.

3. Tom Corbett, "Patron-Driven Acquisitions in School Libraries: The Promise and the Problems," in *Patron-Driven Acquisitions: History and Best Practices*, ed. David A. Swords, 95–105 (Berlin: Walter De Gruyter, 2011).

4. William H. Walters, "Patron-Driven Acquisition and the Educational Mission of the Academic Library," *Library Resources and Technical Services* 56, no. 3 (July 2012): 199–213.

5. Gail Herrera and Judy Greenwood, "Patron-Initiated Purchasing: Evaluating Criteria and Workflows," *Journal of Interlibrary Loan, Document Delivery, and Electronic Reserves* 21, no. 1/2 (2011): 9–24.

6. Michael Kelley, "Librarians Feel Sticker Shock as Price for Random House Ebooks Rises as Much as 300 Percent," *The Digital Shift* (March 2, 2012), www.thedigitalshift.com/2012/03/ebooks/librarians-feel-sticker-shock-as-price-for-random-house-ebooks-rise-as-much-as-300-percent.

7. Andrew Albanese, "Survey Says Library Users Are Your Best Customers," *Publishers Weekly* (Oct. 28, 2011), www.publishersweekly.com/pw/by-topic/industry-news/publishing-and-marketing/article/49316-survey-says-library-users-are-your-best-customers.html.

8. Primary Research Group, *Library Use of EBooks, 2012 Edition* (New York: Primary Research Group, 2011).

9. Lauren Barack, "A Kindle Program of Their Own: Second Graders Try Out Ereaders, Courtesy of Librarian Kathy Parker," *School Library Journal* 56, no. 12 (Dec. 2010): 12; Dennis T. Clark, "Lending Kindle E-book Readers: First Results from the Texas A&M Project," *Collection Building* 28, no. 4 (2009): 146–49; Blaise Derks, "The River Forest Public Library Experience with the Kindle," in *No Shelf Required: E-Books in Libraries*, ed. Sue Polanka, 68–69 (Chicago: American Library Association, 2011); Richard E. Sapon-White, "Kindles and Kindle E-books in an Academic Library," *Library Resources and Technical Services* 56, no. 1 (Jan. 2012): 45–52; Sian Waterfield, *Libraries Loaning E-book Readers* (Cambridge, ON, Canada: Cambridge Libraries and Galleries, 2012).

10. George H. Pike, "First Sale Doctrine Put to the Test," *Information Today* 24, no. 9 (Oct. 2007): 17–19.

11. Christopher Harris, "Ebooks and School Libraries: Schools Face Unique Challenges in Their Efforts to Offer Digital Texts," *American Libraries* (Jan. 13, 2012), http://americanlibraries magazine.org/features/01132012/ebooks-and-school-libraries.

12. Primary Research Group, *Library Use of eBooks, 2012 Edition*

13. Ibid.

14. Primary Research Group, *Survey of Scholarly Journal Licensing and Acquisition Practices, 2012 Edition.* (New York: Primary Research Group, 2012).

15. Ann McKee, Margaret Donahue Walter, and Jose Luis Andrade, presenters, "Shaping, Streamlining, and Solidifying the Information Chain in Turbulent Times," *Serials Librarian* 62, no. 1/4 (2012): 103–11.

16. Stephen Bosch, Patricia A. Promis, and Chris Sugnet, *Guide to Licensing and Acquiring Electronic Information*, Collection Management and Development Guides 13 (Chicago: Association for Library Collections and Technical Services; Lanham, MD: Scarecrow, 2005), 41.

CHAPTER 4
LICENSES FOR E-CONTENT

ENTIRE BOOKS HAVE BEEN written and workshops given that address the process of reviewing and negotiating agreements to acquire and access e-content. By necessity, this chapter is an introduction to this complex topic and explains why these agreements are important, identifies key license elements, and suggests best practices for libraries engaged in negotiating contracts and licenses.

LICENSE TERMINOLOGY

Terminology is a good place to begin. A license (sometimes called a licensing agreement) grants permission to do something which, without such permission, would be illegal. A license for e-content is a contract that presents the terms under which a vendor, publisher, or distributor grants access to a library or sells content to a library. A contract is a formal, legally binding, written agreement between two or more parties. Failure to fulfill the terms of the license is called a breach. A major or persistent breach of contract can result in penalties, which might be a fine, immediate termination, a lawsuit, or all three.

Licenses for e-content are matters of contract law and take priority over copyright law. Once a license is signed, fair use and other rights granted under copyright law are superseded by the terms of the contract. Thus, for example, the doctrine of first sale (section 109 of the U.S. Copyright Act), which permits libraries to lend materials once ownership has transferred to the library, does not necessarily apply to e-content, particularly if the library is not purchasing the content but only paying for the right to access it for a period of time.[1] Licensing and DRM systems have shifted the focus from reliance on copyright laws to the provisions of the license that determine what can be done with the e-content. DRM systems serve to enforce and sometimes extend the scope of the license.

The legal environment is complex because of constantly changing technologies, new business models, and new offerings from vendors, publishers, and distributors. Libraries are challenged to make the best deal possible when negotiating e-resource licenses.

Heavy and increasing user demand for e-content puts pressures on libraries to provide as much as possible and as quickly as possible. A valuable website for librarians seeking to learn more about licensing is LIBLICENSE (http://liblicense.crl.edu). This site provides resources, including model license language, a model license, and detailed discussion of licensing terms. Another resource is LicensingModels.org (www.licensingmodels.org). This site offers six model licenses for use by publishers, librarians, and subscription agents for electronic resources. The licenses are designed for use by a single academic institution, academic consortia, public libraries, and corporate and other special libraries. In addition, it provides model licenses for e-book and journal archive purchases and licenses for a thirty- or sixty-day free trial.

IMPORTANCE OF LICENSES

Licenses for e-content are legally binding agreements enforceable by law. That fact alone should make clear their importance. The licensor can ask whatever price and set whatever conditions on use the licensee will accept. Signing a license binds the signatories to comply with all obligations set out in its clauses. A library should ensure that the conditions placed on it and its users are not onerous. By signing the license, the individual who does so is committing the library to abide by it.

Licensed e-content is not covered by the fair use provisions of U.S. copyright law. A library will find that licenses frequently prohibit many of the uses (circulating, placing on reserve for a course, providing through ILL, etc.) it has traditionally made of its materials. Understanding what is prohibited and permitted in a license is essential.

Licenses have consequences if the obligations specified in them are not met. If a library exceeds the activities agreed on or the approved uses specifically set forth in the license, it is in breach of the license. Failure to meet obligations can result in fines or termination of access. Understanding these consequences is critical, as is deciding if they are acceptable.

In private life, individuals are constantly advised never to sign an agreement before reading it carefully and understanding what it entails. Libraries signing licenses for e-content should follow this advice no less rigorously.

KEY ELEMENTS IN LICENSES

Licenses usually begin with definitions, followed by clauses that lay out the terms of the license, attachments, and finally signatures by those authorized to sign contracts on behalf of the licensor and licensee.

Definitions, which identify all potentially disputable terms, usually appear first in a license. Two important definitions explain what is meant by authorized user(s) or authorized patron(s) and authorized site(s). Authorized users are those individuals authorized under the contract to use, access, or download the product. The authorized site is the location where the licensee provides access to the e-content. Licenses that govern downloading of e-content to handheld devices generally do not include a definition of authorized site. Additionally, the e-content or product is defined. For example, a contract for e-books downloadable to personal devices might state, "*Content* shall consist of digital files and titles available for loan to patrons at the licensor's website."

Terms specify the rights and responsibilities of the licensor and licensee. Most licenses have standard elements, although the manner in which each issue is addressed can vary. The type of e-content (e.g., databases, e-books, media) covered by the license also can affect the clauses and their terms. Usual elements in licenses speak to

- delivery and access, including authentication
- authorized uses, including any restrictions on use
- licensor obligations
- licensee obligations
- term of the agreement, including processes for renewal and early termination
- warranties, indemnities, and limitations on warranties
- governing law and dispute resolution
- nondisclosure
- force majeure
- fees and payment

Delivery and Access

A clause found in nearly all licenses addresses how the content will be delivered and accessed, often via remote access to the licensor's server from which it can be viewed and downloaded in whole or part. In some cases, the licensee receives the content and houses it in a local server for user access. Authentication is the process that verifies the identities of users before access is granted. Common methods of authentication are passwords and user IDs, library cards, IP addresses and secure proxy servers, public keys, digital certificates, and federated authentication protocols such as Shibboleth. In 2011, the National Information Standards Organization published *ESPReSSO: Establishing Suggested Practices Regarding Single Sign-On,* which recommends solutions for improving the use of single sign-on technologies to ensure a seamless experience for users.[2] *ESPReSSO* aims to mitigate the growing complexity of licensing situations and network design and the increasing use of mobiles devices, which have created a confusing and error-prone environment for users, licensors, and service providers.

A subset of licenses for e-content is that for media, which often includes a particularly restrictive set of access principles unfavorable to instruction and research. This is especially the case when licensing online, on-demand video and music with their associated intellectual property concerns. Music and film rights owners generally have not settled on a business model for granting distribution rights to distributors. Image licensing tends to be less restrictive, and some vendors offer reasonable terms and conditions. Most distributors of on-demand video license access to individual titles for a fixed term (usually one to five years). Renewal of the license is generally dependent on the distributor's contractual terms and arrangements with the filmmaker.

Authorized Use

Authorized uses and restrictions on use define the rights granted or denied under the license. By contract law, any rights not expressly granted in the license are reserved to the licensor. Typical rights granted to the licensee are users' rights to search, browse, retrieve, view, display, download, print results, and store or save the content for a specific period. Some licenses do not permit printing of any content and may have DRM systems in place that disable cut-and-paste. Rights granted may include, for example, users' ability to forward an e-journal article electronically to themselves or to other persons. Restrictions may include a limit on the number of times an e-book can circulate or may limit circulation to a single user at a time (the "one book, one reader" model). Most contracts explicitly prohibit copying substantial portions of a database or a single book, downloading or printing entire issues of a journal, modifying search software or content, or disabling the DRM system. Authorized use may be restricted to, for example, academic, scholarly, or noncommercial use. Some academic libraries are seeking to add the ability of authorized users to perform text or data mining for academic research and other educational purposes.

Academic libraries often seek the right to use the product in ILL transactions, distance education, course packs, course reserves, and course management systems. These rights are, however, often prohibited in licenses and, in addition, may be limited by the DRM system controlling the product. Thus, even though libraries do get fair use rights under the U.S. Copyright Act to lend items to other libraries under certain conditions, the DRM-protected files and license terms, which take precedence, mean that libraries often cannot exercise the rights granted by law. A typical clause authorizing ILL might state, "The Licensee may supply to another library at the request of a patron thereof (whether by post, fax, or secure transmission), for the purposes of research or private study and not for commercial use, a single paper copy of an electronic original of an individual document being part of the Licensed Content." Note that this authorized use requires using a paper copy of the e-content for ILL. At this point, few licensors permit ILL of e-books and many prohibit its use for course reserves. At the time of this writing, Springer was one of the few publishers offering an option with ILL privileges. Project MUSE, which began adding university press books in 2011, permits using a single copy of an individual e-book chapter in response to an ILL request.[3] Restricting ILL can be of concern for consortia that seek to increase the number of titles available to their members with fewer copies of a single title held locally.

The licensor may reserve the right to modify services and content with or without notification. A typical clause might state that the licensor reserves the right at any time to withdraw any title, item, or part of an item for which it no longer retains the right to publish, or which it has reasonable grounds to believe infringes copyrights or is defamatory, obscene, unlawful, or otherwise objectionable. This means that the licensor can remove, replace, edit, or modify content. Libraries are familiar with the frequency with which aggregators of e-journals add and remove titles. Aggregators of e-books may remove a title at the request of the copyright holder. For example, Amazon deleted some digital editions of George Orwell's *Animal Farm* and *1984* from Kindles of readers who had bought the books.[4] Even more troubling to libraries is the ability to modify the original text without notification or use of tracking, versioning, archiving, or other means that might provide access to the original content.

Obligations

Licensor obligations always should include providing the content that is being licensed. Other frequent obligations are training library employees, providing technical and perhaps user support as well as documentation, replacing defective products, guaranteeing hours of access and service, hosting a website customized to the library and the product, providing use statistics, and protecting the privacy of users.

Protecting user privacy is a long-standing principle and value in libraries and often mandated by state confidentiality laws and library privacy policies. The American Library Association states that "privacy is essential to the exercise of free speech, free thought, and free association" and that, "in a library (physical or virtual), the right to privacy is the right to open inquiry without having the subject of one's interest examined or scrutinized by others."[5] In fall 2011, libraries learned that their users who loaded e-books provided by Over-Drive onto Kindles were being tracked by Amazon. When the loan period for an e-book on a Kindle was nearly over, Kindle users received messages from Amazon asking if they wanted to buy the e-book. Although OverDrive did not track or provide user information, Amazon required users to log in with their Kindle accounts to access the borrowed book, which Amazon then used for marketing. Some libraries responded by posting notices to their users that using a Kindle to download e-books took them away from the libraries' privacy policies. OverDrive's terms and conditions reference the OverDrive privacy policy, which states:

> OverDrive may also use and share non-personally identifiable information, such as general demographic or location information, or information about the computer or device from which you access the Services. Additionally, we may anonymize personal Information and share it in an aggregated form with third parties, advertisers and/or business partners in order to analyze service usage, improve the OverDrive service and your experience, or for other similar purposes. The use and disclosure of such information is not subject to any restrictions under this privacy policy.[6]

Carefully reviewing the OverDrive license would suggest that users' privacy is protected, but the OverDrive license does not cover Amazon behavior. Caldwell-Stone observed, "Libraries, anxious to provide users with a popular, in-demand service, did so without carefully evaluating the service's impact on user privacy."[7] She advises libraries to examine agreements and the technologies and platforms that control delivery of e-content thoroughly.

Of increasing importance is a licensor obligation to provide supporting assistive software or devices designed to comply with the requirements of the Americans with Disabilities Act.[8] An important source are the "Web Content Accessibility Guidelines" published by the World Wide Web Consortium.[9]

Additionally, libraries often seek to obligate licensors of e-books to provide MARC records for loading into a local catalog. This obligation specifies the library's expectations for quality, accuracy, format, and currency of these records. If the library is required to pay for the records, this is specified in the fees section of the contract.

Licensee obligations generally address the level and type of security the library must provide to ensure that only authorized users can access the content and that use is limited to that authorized under the license's terms. The licensor's intent is to protect intellectual property interests. Libraries should not promise to prevent all misuse (as defined in the license) of the product, but they can agree to take reasonable and appropriate measures to prevent it, notify the user community of all restrictions, and carry out due process when a user violates the license. The library may be obligated to keep appropriate documentation regarding practices in place and provide the licensor access to validate total number of downloads.

Term of the Agreement

The clause dealing with the term of the license (sometimes called duration of grant of rights) lays out when the agreement becomes effective and its duration, which may or may not match the term of the subscription. This section usually includes the processes for renewal and early termination. Many licenses contain a provision for automatic renewal unless either party gives written notice of intent not to renew. Usually this notification must be given a set number of days before the expiration of the current term. The section dealing with early termination specifies under what conditions the contract can be terminated, which might be licensor or licensee failure to fulfill obligations or deception in the warranties. For example, the licensor may specify immediate termination of access in the case of a security breach. Libraries usually ask for a cure period (often thirty days) in which to remedy or correct any breach. Libraries may negotiate adding a clause that permits early cancellation in the case of financial exigency.

An important concern for most libraries is the issue of continuing access to the content when the license is terminated or the licensor ceases to offer the product. Unlike subscriptions to print publications, a library does not automatically get to keep the e-product to which it had access during the term of the license. The section dealing with the term of the license may address this, or it may be dealt with elsewhere. Ideally, a license should include provision for affordable, perpetual access to the licensed content by some appropriate and feasible means. Some licenses may grant the library the right to make and save a copy of the content during the duration of the contract or permission to create backup copies for preservation purposes, but this places the onus on the library to have storage and access mechanisms in place either on-site or through a service provider. An example clause might state, "On termination of this License, the Licensor shall provide continuing access for library staff and patrons to that part of the Licensed Materials which was published and paid for within the subscription period, either from the Licensor's server or by supplying electronic files to the Licensee, except where such termination is due to a breach of the License by the Licensee that the Licensee has failed to remedy." If a license agreement does not permit the licensee to make a preservation copy, a license agreement should specify who has permanent archival responsibility for the resource and under what conditions the licensee may access or refer users to the archival copy. Some publishers provide perpetual access through archiving programs such as LOCKSS, CLOCKSS, or POR-TICO to ensure that the content remains available if the publisher ceases the publication or goes out of business.

The question of e-content ownership at the termination of an agreement was the topic of a 2011 dispute when the State Library of Kansas opted not to renew its contract with OverDrive, through which 330 public libraries across Kansas accessed e-books.[10] OverDrive proposed a contract renewal that would have increased administrative fees for the platform from $10,000 to $75,000 a year by 2014. Jo Budler, director of the State Library of Kansas, noted that the new agreement also removed language that recognized the library's ownership of materials and its right to transfer content to another service provider. When further negotiations with OverDrive failed to reach an acceptable agreement, Budler did not renew the contract. She enlisted the support of Jeff Chanay, the Kansas deputy attorney general for the civil litigation division, who took the position that the State Library owned the content. The State Library then contracted with 3M for its Cloud Library e-book service and began seeking permission from 169 publishers to move the e-books to the new services without having to pay a new fee. Most publishers have agreed with this request. Although libraries will not likely find themselves in the same situation, this dispute makes clear the importance of carefully reading licenses, including revisions presented at the point of renewal.

OPTIONS FOR PERPETUAL ACCESS

Portico (www.portico.org) is a nonprofit digital preservation service provided by ITHAKA that maintains a permanent archive of electronic scholarly journals and books. Participating libraries are provided with campus-wide access to archived content when specific trigger events occur, including when titles are no longer available from the publisher or other source. Portico also provides a reliable means to secure perpetual access when a participating publisher chooses to designate Portico as a provider of post-cancellation access. Participating libraries make an annual support payment based on their total library materials expenditures.

LOCKSS (Lots of Copies Keep Stuff Safe, www.lockss.org), a nonprofit service under the auspices of Stanford University, develops and supports an open-source system for digital preservation that allows libraries to collect, preserve, and provide their users with access to e-content. It operates on a distributed network of preservation appliances (called LOCKSS Boxes) and allows libraries to collect, store, preserve, and provide access to their own, local copies of e-content. LOCKSS is a "light" archive—the content is currently accessible under the terms of applicable licenses. Each library's system collects a copy using a specialized web crawler that verifies that the publisher has granted suitable permission. Libraries that have collected the same material cooperate in a peer-to-peer network to ensure its preservation and a high degree of replication. Each library is responsible for creating its local LOCKSS Box, installing the open-source software, and maintaining the hardware and software. LOCKSS aims to provide 100 percent post-cancellation access.

CLOCKSS (Controlled LOCKSS, www.clockss.org) builds on the LOCKSS technology and directly engages scholarly publishers in preservation of their digital output in a "dark" archive of geographically dispersed nodes at fifteen major research libraries. Content preserved in CLOCKSS can be accessed only when a trigger event is deemed to have occurred. CLOCKSS makes all content triggered from the archive freely available to the world. Libraries and publishers pay an annual fee to participate.

Warranties, Indemnities, and Limitations on Warranties

Warranties are promises made by parties to the license. The licensor may guarantee hours of access or server performance for a remote resource. Another typical warranty is assurance that the licensor legally owns the copyright to or the content of the product. Indemnification is one party's agreement to insure, shield, or otherwise defend another party against third-party claims resulting from performance under the agreement. A warranty guarantees the rights, and the indemnity provides for financial compensation should the warranty prove false. Libraries should seek license agreements that require the licensor to defend, indemnify, and hold the licensee harmless from any action based on a claim that use of the resource in accordance with the license infringes any patent, copyright, trademark, or trade secret of any third party; in other words, the licensor affirms that it has legal right to use the content provided. This ensures that the library cannot be accused of copyright infringements as long as use abides by the license terms.

A licensor may ask a library to indemnify the licensor against misuse or abuse by the library's authorized users. Libraries generally should not accept a clause requiring indemnification against misuse by its patrons; many public institutions in the United States are prohibited from indemnifying licensors or holding them harmless to other parties. A library may agree elsewhere in the license to take all reasonable and appropriate measures to protect the licensed product from misuse, but it should avoid promising that its users will never abuse their rights. A license should require the licensor to give the library notice of suspected or alleged license violations that come to the licensor's attention and to allow a reasonable time for the library to investigate and take corrective action, if needed.

A limit of liability clause sets out how much and what kind of damages will be paid for remedies. Penalties are applied when contractual obligations are breached. For example, a library may be charged a penalty fee for late payment. Access may be withheld until the breach is resolved.

Governing Law and Dispute Resolution

Governing law identifies the state or country (venue) and its laws under which a dispute relating to the license will be adjudicated. Libraries usually negotiate for jurisdiction in the state in which they are located; a licensor usually prefers the state or country in which its primary office is located. A compromise revision might state that cases will be adjudicated in the courts of the state in which the claim is brought.

Nondisclosure

A nondisclosure agreement (sometimes called a confidentiality clause) is a provision in a license in which the parties agree to refrain from disclosing or making public certain information outside a mutually agreeable scope. Such nondisclosure clauses often prohibit the library from sharing information about the price being paid to purchase or access the content or details about how the price is determined. The licensor may promise a lower cost if the library agrees not to share pricing information; it may state that finalizing a contract is contingent on accepting the nondisclosure provision. However, mandated confidentiality hampers effective negotiations if libraries do not know what other libraries are paying or details involved in determining cost. The International Coalition of Library Consortia issued a statement in 2004 on preferred practices that states "non-disclosure language should not be required for any licensing agreement, particularly language that would preclude library consortia from sharing pricing and other significant terms and conditions with other consortia."[11] In 2009, the Association of Research Libraries board of directors approved a resolution that strongly encourages its member libraries to refrain from signing agreements with publishers or vendors, either individually or through consortia, that include nondisclosure or confidentiality clauses.[12] Nondisclosure clauses are not considered a deal breaker in all libraries, but some libraries are mandated either by law or policy to make this information public upon request and cannot accept a nondisclosure condition. Libraries benefit from knowing what their peers were able to negotiate in both the terms governing a specific product and the fees charged for it.

Force Majeure

Force majeure means that neither party shall be found at fault to the extent that performance of obligations or attempts to cure any breach are delayed or prevented by reasons of any act of God, natural disaster, accident, act of government, shortages of materials or supplies, or any other causes beyond the control of such party.

Fees and Payment

The section on fees and payments lays out the cost, how it is determined, and a payment schedule. Fees can vary widely. The final price is determined by the business model selected and the results of negotiation. The business model may be one book/one user, a set number of simultaneous users, unlimited simultaneous use, subscription, patron-driven acquisitions, or pay-per-view charged to the library or, more rarely, the user. It may be based on the number of users, size of the institution, or number of transactions (which may be logins, searches, downloads, etc.). Fees may include system, access, and hosting fees or a fee to provide a customized, hosted website through which users access the content. Some suppliers calculate annual fees based on existing collection use data. If a library inadvertently leases a title that suddenly becomes popular, the charge may be more after the sale.

Attachments and Signature Page

Licenses frequently contain supplementary documents, called attachments. These generally set the terms of payment or payment schedule. They may list titles included in a package. For example, a license may define the product by referencing the details provided in an attachment. Attachments are legally part of the license and equally binding.

The final element in a license is the section where it is signed and dated by authorized representatives of the licensor and the licensee. The signature must be provided by a person with authority and power to represent and legally bind a party to a written contract. In some instances, an individual signing a license beyond his or her authority may be held personally liable for enforcing the license or paying damages if the license is breached.

BEST PRACTICES

After slogging through the key elements in licenses, the reader may wonder if legal training is a requirement to understanding and negotiating licenses. The simple answer is no. Having a familiarity with the terms and their meaning is generally sufficient for most license negotiations. Additionally, some publishers and content providers have found repeated negotiations with multiple libraries on the same points to be less than efficient use of their time. They are becoming more comfortable with libraries' commitment to and ability to protect intellectual property. One promising development is SERU: Shared Electronic Resource Understanding, a best practice of the U.S. National Information Standards Organization (NISO).

The NISO SERU website (www.niso.org/workrooms/seru) offers resources for libraries, consortia, and publishers to reduce the use of licensing agreements and the amount of time negotiating licenses. SERU was originally designed to replace licenses for e-journals and has been expanded to accommodate journal backfiles and e-books. Under SERU, no license is required because U.S. copyright law governs use. SERU is not legally binding but instead is a collection of statements to which the licensor and the licensee agree. To implement SERU, an organization must sign up to be added to the SERU registry (available on the SERU website), which lists publishers and content providers, libraries, and consortia that are interested in applying SERU to some products.

Even when a license is required, libraries following the bests practice presented here should be able to navigate through the licensing process effectively. Libraries should begin by developing their own guidelines for acceptable licenses. These will serve as an internal guide or checklist for the library to follow when reviewing and negotiating a license and ensure a consistent approach to negotiating all licenses. The guidelines should identify any mandated clauses, clauses that the library is prohibited from accepting, and clauses that are preferred but not mandatory. Points raised in each of the key elements presented in the previous section can inform the guidelines. A few that merit special attention are

- definition of authorized users
- library rights to use the content for ILL, distance education, and course reserves
- user rights to print, download, e-mail, or copy and paste content
- notification of modification to services and content
- rights to perpetual access
- confidentiality of users
- applicable governing law
- provision of use statistics
- indemnification
- renewal and termination processes
- preferred payment scheme and awareness of what the library is prepared to pay

Libraries should make decisions on these points and set acceptable baselines that are consistent with their mission and with the legal environment in which they operate.

Other points that might appear on a checklist address the library's ability to meet license obligations as well as conditions associated with accessing the content. Can the library authenticate authorized users as required? Can the library commit to taking the appropriate and reasonable measures to ensure that the content is not misused? Is the library able to provide additional hardware and software if it is needed? Is content accessible from the handheld devices most users own? Reviewing these points with the proposed license in hand is essential to protect the library and to make certain patrons can access the content.

Implicit in the development and use of a checklist is the provision of a written license against which the checklist is compared. Libraries should insist on a written license and review it attentively. The license binds the licensor in writing just as it binds the licensee—the library.

Determining who should negotiate on behalf of the library and request amendments to the license is vital. This responsibility is usually limited to a single individual. This person might be someone in the library (e.g., collections development librarian or officer, librarian working in acquisitions, electronic resources librarian, digital library manager, library director) or someone from the office of legal counsel or purchasing unit of the parent organization. Negotiation might take place at the consortial level by someone empowered to act on behalf of the consortium and thus its members. Often, if an attorney is not involved in the negotiations, the library may refer the final license to the library's attorney or that of its parent organization for final wording and approval. The individual designated for license negotiations should be authorized to reject offers and terminate the license negotiation if mutually acceptable agreement cannot be reached.

The individual who negotiates on behalf of the library may not be the person who is authorized to sign the license. The individual who signs the contract must have the authority to bind the library to, approve, or execute a contract on the library's behalf. Many libraries operate under clear delegations and subdelegations of authority. In some, only the library director has the delegated authority to bind the library to a legally enforceable obligation. He or she may have subdelegated the authority to someone else in the library. In other libraries, this authority to sign licenses may be reserved to an individual at an upper level in the parent organization.

Once a license is signed by the participating parties, the library needs a process in place to manage it. This means a mechanism to track the terms and conditions, product costs, and renewal process. Maintaining paper files quickly becomes onerous. Libraries may develop an in-house ERM database to track their licenses or may purchase a commercial ERM product often linked to an ILS. ERM systems facilitate managing the life cycle of license agreements. Data entered and tracked usually include the licensor, name of the product, effective date of the license, expiration date, and terms of use rights and restrictions in the license. Some libraries use the ERM to hyperlink to a scanned image of the license stored digitally on a server. Some libraries create separate online files that track, by product, rights to use (or not) its content for ILL, course reserves, and distance education.

SHORTLIST OF BEST LICENSING PRACTICES

- Have a checklist of your library's requirements and compare all clauses in a license to these requirements.
- Require a written license.
- Read the license carefully and understand all aspects.
- Pay particular attention to access and use rights.
- Know what you can pay.
- Determine who can negotiate on behalf of the library.
- Be prepared to negotiate and to walk away if agreement cannot be reached.
- Ensure that the individual signing the license has legal authority to do so.
- When you have questions or if required by local practice, consult the legal counsel for your library.
- Retain and manage licenses after signature.

SUMMARY

Licenses for e-content are matters of contract law and take priority over copyright law. They are legally binding agreements enforceable by law. Licenses have consequences if the obligations specified in them are not met. Understanding what is prohibited and permitted in a license is essential. Two areas of particular concern to libraries are the definition of authorized users and of the rights granted to the library and its users. These rights spell out what is and what is not permitted. Equally important are obligations placed on both the licensor and the library.

Many licenses address the same issues in similar clauses and with similar vocabulary. Understanding these issues, clauses, and legal terms facilitates successfully negotiating and finalizing a license that is acceptable to both the licensor and the library. Developing a set of guidelines or a checklist of areas to monitor is valuable. The guidelines identify any mandated clauses that must be present, any that the library is prohibited from accepting, and any that are preferred but not mandatory. Libraries are advised to track licenses through their life cycle because of their legally binding nature and the consequences of failing to meet obligations.

Suggested Readings

Albitz, Becky. *Licensing and Managing Electronic Resources.* Oxford, UK: Chandos, 2008.

American Association of Law Libraries. "Principles for Licensing Electronic Resources." (Nov. 2004). www.aallnet.org/main-menu/Advocacy/recommendedguidelines/licensing -electronic-resources.html.

Ashmore, Beth, Jill E. Grogg, and Jeff Weddle. *The Librarian's Guide to Negotiation: Winning Strategies for the Digital Age.* Medford, NJ: Information Today, 2012.

Brown, Kincaid C. "Tactics and Terms in the Negotiation of Electronic Resource Licenses." In *Electronic Resource Management in Libraries: Research and Practice,* ed. Holly Yu and Scott Breivold, 174–92. Hershey, PA: Information Science Reference, 2008.

Davis, Trisha, and Celeste Feather. "The Evolution of License Content." In *Electronic Resource Management in Libraries: Research and Practice,* ed. Holly Yu and Scott Breivold, 123–44. Hershey, PA: Information Science Reference, 2008.

Dougherty, William C. "Managing Technology: The Copyright Quagmire." *Journal of Academic Librarianship* 36, no. 4 (July 2010): 351–53.

Eschenfelder, Kristin. "Every Library's Nightmare? Digital Rights Management, Use Restrictions, and Licensed Scholarly Digital Resources." *College and Research Libraries* 69, no. 3 (May 2008): 205–25.

Fogden, Fiona. "Negotiation of Contracts: Planning for the Unknown with Boilerplate Clauses." *Legal Information Management* 11, no. 1 (2011): 27–31.

Frederiksen, Linda, et al. "Ebooks and Interlibrary Loan: Licensed to Fill?" *Interlibrary Loan, Document Delivery and Electronic Reserve* 21, no. 3 (2011): 117–31.

Grogg, Jill E., and Selden Durgom Lamoureux. "Issues in E-resource Licensing." In *Managing the Transition from Print to Electronic Journals and Resources: A Guide for Library and Information Professionals,* ed. Maria D. D. Collins and Patrick L. Carr, 273–85. New York: Routledge, 2008.

Hamaker, Charles. "What's New in Licensing Electronic Resources for Libraries?" *Searcher* 19, no. 5 (June 2011): 32–36.

Handman, Gary. "License to Look: Evolving Models for Library Video Acquisition and Access." *Library Trends* 58, no. 3 (Winter 2010): 324–34.

Harris, Lesley Ellen. *Licensing Digital Content: A Practical Guide for Librarians.* 2nd ed. Chicago: American Library Association, 2009.

———. "Striving for Consistency in Your Digital Content Licensing Policy." *Information Outlook* 12, no. 4 (Apr. 2008): 38–39.

International Federation of Library Associations and Institutions. "Licensing Principles (2001)." www.ifla.org/V/ebpb/copy.htm.

Kovacs, Diane K. "E-resource Licensing Basics: Getting What You Need for What You Are Willing to Pay." In *The Kovacs Guide to Electronic Library Collection Development,* 2nd ed., 83–107. New York: Neal-Schuman, 2009.

Lamoureux, Selden Durgom, Clint Chamberlain, and Jane Bethel. "Basics of E-resource Licensing." *Serials Librarian* 58, no. 1/4 (Apr. 2010): 20–31.

Lamoureux, Selden Durgom, and James Stemper. "White Paper: Trends in Licensing." *Research Library Issues* no. 275 (June 2011): 19–24.

Levine-Clark, Michael. "Whither ILL? Wither ILL: The Changing Nature of Resource Sharing for E-books." *Collaborative Librarianship* 3, no. 2 (2011): 71–72.

O'Brien, David R., Urs Gasser, and John Palfrey. *E-books in Libraries: A Briefing Document Developed in Preparation for a Workshop on E-lending in Libraries,* Berkman Center Research Publication 20012–15. Boston: Berkman Center for Internet and Society at Harvard University, 2012. http://ssrn.com/abstract=2111396.

Soules, Aline, and Donna L. Ferullo. "Copyright Implications for Electronic Resources." In *Electronic Resource Management in Libraries: Research and Practice,* ed. Holly Yu and Scott Breivold, 145–69. Hershey, PA: Information Science Reference, 2008.

Upshall, Michael. *Content Licensing: Buying and Selling Digital Resources.* Oxford, UK: Chandos, 2009.

Wicht, Heather. "The Evolution of E-books and Interlibrary Loan in Academic Libraries." *Collaborative Librarianship* 3, no. 4 (2011): 205–11.

Notes

1. U.S. Copyright Act, Public Law 94–553, U.S. Statutes at Large 90 (1976): 2541, codified at 17 U.S.C. §107.
2. National Information Standards Organization, *ESPReSSO: Establishing Suggested Practices Regarding Single Sign-On,* NISO RP-11–20111 (Baltimore: NISO, 2011), www.niso.org/publications/rp/RP-11–2011_ESPReSSO.pdf.
3. Project MUSE, "UPCC Books Frequently Asked Questions," http://muse.jhu.edu/about/faq_books.html#top.
4. Brad Stone, "Amazon Erases Orwell Books from Kindle," New York Times (July 17, 2009), www.nytimes.com/2009/07/18/technology/companies/18amazon.html.
5. American Library Association, Privacy, "An Interpretation of the Library Bill of Rights" (June 2002), www.ala.org/advocacy/intfreedom/librarybill/interpretations/privacy.
6. OverDrive, "Privacy Policy," www.overdrive.com/privacypolicy.aspx.
7. Deborah Caldwell-Stone, "A Digital Dilemma: Ebooks and Users' Rights," *American Libraries* (May 5, 2012), http://americanlibrariesmagazine.org/features/05292012/digital-dilemma-ebooks-and-users-rights.
8. Americans with Disabilities Act, Public Law 101–336, 101st Cong. (July 26, 1990); ADA Amendments Act of 2008, Public Law 110–325, 110th Cong. (Sept. 25, 2008).
9. W3C, "Web Content Accessibility Guidelines (WCAG) 2.0: W3C Recommendation 11 December 2008," www.w3.org/TR/2008/REC-WCAG20-20081211/.
10. Michael Kelley, "Kansas State Librarian Argues Consortium Owns, Not Licenses, Content from OverDrive," *Library Journal* (June 20, 2011), www.libraryjournal.com/lj/home/891052-264/kansas_state_librarian_argues.html.csp; Jo Budler, Kansas State Librarian, "Open Letter to Kansas Librarians" (Oct. 12, 2011), www.kslib.info/Documents/digital%20books/

joletter091211.pdf; Michael Kelley, "Kansas State Librarian Can Transfer Thousands of Titles from OverDrive to 3M at No Charge," *Library Journal* (Oct. 2011), www.libraryjournal.com/lj/home/892348-264/kansas_state_librarian_can_transfer.html.csp.

11. International Coalition of Library Consortia, "Statement of Current Perspective and Preferred Practice for Selection and Purchase of Electronic Information: Update No. 2, Pricing and Economics" (Oct. 2004), http://icolc.net/statement/statement-current-perspective-and-preferred-practices-selection-and-purchase-electronic.

12. Association of Research Libraries, "ARL Encourages Members to Refrain from Signing Nondisclosure of Confidentiality Clauses" (June 5, 2009), www.arl.org/news/pr/nondisclosure-5june09.shtml.

CHAPTER 5

CONDUCTING BUSINESS WITH E-CONTENT AND SERVICE SUPPLIERS

ALL LIBRARIES WORK with content suppliers—publishers, aggregators, vendors, subscription agents, or an entity that provides a combination of the products and services normally associated with one of these suppliers. Some libraries work with many types of content suppliers and with multiple companies in each of these categories. Other libraries work with a more limited number of suppliers. The librarian's responsibility is to obtain the best deal possible—one that results in cost-effective services and e-content that meet users' need and satisfy the library's goals. An important element in obtaining this aim is building and maintaining effective relationships. This chapter explores aspects of library relations with e-content and service suppliers: researching suppliers and service providers, negotiating successfully, and communicating effectively throughout the course of their relationship.

RESEARCHING SUPPLIERS AND SERVICE PROVIDERS

A relationship with a content or service supplier begins with researching possibilities and options. The first question to be answered is whether the supplier offers the e-content and services in which the library is interested. The next question is whether the supplier's business model meets the library's needs. To find answers, librarians collect information on products, prices, and services that have been determined of interest.

Informal Sources of Information

Librarians can obtain information about the products and services offered by publishers, vendors, agents, and aggregators in various ways. A good place to begin is at their websites, which also may give a hint to the functionality of their interfaces. Librarians can also gather information by visiting exhibitors' booths and meeting with content and services suppliers at professional conferences and meetings. Most content suppliers have sales representatives who visit libraries and are happy to discuss their products and services. The challenge for the librarian is to ensure that the representative clearly understands when the conversation is intended to provide facts and when it shifts to a sales call.

Many librarians consult with colleagues to learn about their experiences, both positive and negative, with e-content providers. These informal conversations can be enlightening. Even if a nondisclosure license clause, which usually governs the sharing of pricing and business models, is in effect, librarians may be able to talk in hypothetical terms and discuss the variety and quality of products and services offered.

Professional journals such as *Library Journal, American Libraries,* and *Against the Grain* regularly compare suppliers and their offerings and provide industry news. *Library Hi Tech News* covers developments in library automation, vendor products, network news, and software and hardware. *Library Technology Reports* also covers library systems and services. *The Digital Shift* (www.thedigitalshift.com) is an online site that posts timely technology-related articles published by *Library Journal* and *School Library Journal.*[1]

An important topic to research is the supplier's financial health. Libraries typically remit funds at the beginning of a subscription, lease, or fiscal or calendar year when contracting with vendors, subscription agents, and aggregators. In return, the library expects a year's worth of content, database access, and service provision. Libraries should be confident that the supplier selected is financially viable. The last major collapse of a serials agent was the bankruptcy of Faxon, which left many libraries in trouble. They had paid for 2003 subscriptions, but Faxon had not paid publishers when bankruptcy was declared. Libraries had to spend months struggling to get the content for which they had paid. Mergers and acquisitions, which are more common corporate changes than bankruptcy, also can create problems for libraries as they and their suppliers learn to work with new representatives, internal systems, and workflows. Monitoring sources such as *Publishers Weekly* and *Publishing Trends* (www.publishingtrends.com), a free monthly online newsletter, can help track publishing news and trends.

Once pertinent information has been assembled, it requires analysis. A typical approach is to create a matrix listing possible suppliers (publishers, aggregators, vendors, agents, etc.) on one axis and key points of comparison on the other axis. Each critical factor (see chapter 3) that will inform the decision should be listed and, to the extent possible, these factors should be comparable across the suppliers. A vendor's or agent's suppliers also may be its competitors; therefore, a library should ensure that the matrix includes all value-added services that it deems of high priority.

Formal Sources of Information

More formal approaches to gathering research are the request for information (RFI), request for proposal (RFP), and request for quotation (RFQ). All require that the library, usually working with the purchasing unit in its parent organization, understand and clearly define its needs in as great detail as possible and assign priorities to these needs. The process of developing an effective RFI, RFP, or RFQ is extremely time-consuming for the library and companies, which usually invest significant funds in developing their responses and presentations. A representative of one major subscription agency noted that his company is becoming more selective in responding to RFPs because of the complexities inherent in the marketplace and a dual print and digital environment.[2] The process of preparing and issuing an RFI, RFP, or RFQ should not be undertaken lightly.

The purpose of an RFI is to collect written information about the capabilities and strengths of various suppliers that will inform the library's decision about which steps to take next. An RFI is not an invitation to bid, nor is it legally binding on either party; it is for informational purposes only. An RFI is designed to elicit information in a manner that facilitates comparison and can be used to populate an assessment matrix. The next step, on receiving the requested information, might be choosing a supplier or issuing an RFP.

An RFP is an official invitation to submit a written proposal to provide a specific product, service, or both. It typically involves and may be issued by the library's purchasing department or that of its parent organization. Many libraries or the entities of which they are a part require RFPs for products and services more than a set dollar amount. RFPs may require competitive bidding, but the lowest price usually is not the single deciding factor. An RFP typically requests information about the supplier's product, services, technical capabilities, and price. Other requested data may include corporate information and qualifications (history, expertise of employees, etc.), evidence of corporate financial stability, and customer references. The RFP is presented to multiple suppliers to review and respond with a proposal.

An RFP should present a formal statement of requirements against which performance can be measured and from which a contract can be written. Preparing an RFP should involve appropriate stakeholders, including but not limited to librarians responsible for selection and acquisitions or serials staff. Developing an RFP requires the library to identify, describe, and prioritize its needs. Having the staff members affected by the final choice participate in the process is essential. If the library has a current supplier to whom the RFP will be issued, staff should be invited to report what works well and what does not in doing business with that company. Requirements are defined as problems needing solutions and should be forward-looking and go beyond a description of the e-content and services provided by a current supplier. The RFP should specify the exact structure and format of the supplier's response and the basis of evaluation criteria. The result of a well-crafted RFP should be a consistent set of vendor responses for easy comparison.

RFPs usually require the respondents to provide copies of their financial statements, report if they are currently for sale or involved in any transaction to be acquired by another business entity, give details of all past or pending litigation, and supply any additional information about their financial stability. RFPs may ask the respondents to describe their company's quality assurance program and how performance is measured. The primary substance of an RFP details the proposal specifications and addresses processes such as ordering, claims, cancellations, renewals, prepayments, billing, invoices, credits, electronic data exchange, and reports. Additional sections ask how communication is handled and the respondent's online database accessed. Respondents may be encouraged to propose solutions that provide process improvements.

RFP PROCESS

The RFP process follows a standard sequence of tasks, usually including the following:

- Consult with the library's purchasing office (or that of the library's parent organization) to ensure compliance with policies and procedures.
- Appoint the task group of stakeholders that will develop the RFP and evaluate responses. Frequently, these stakeholders include representatives with collection development and management,

acquisitions, cataloging, systems, and accounting responsibilities, and, perhaps, someone from the institutional purchasing unit.

- Hold an initial meeting of stakeholders to identify general issues and desired outcomes.
- Conduct a detailed needs analysis and identify features or elements that are required, preferred, and desired.
- Write the RFP based on the needs analysis and features expected in the proposal. Ideally, those writing the RFP can use other RFPs as guides. If the library is using an earlier RFP that it issued, care should be taken to update it.
- Determine how responses will be compared and evaluated. The RFP should be written in a manner that elicits responses that can be scored.
- Identify suppliers to whom to send the RFP.
- Set deadlines for presubmission questions and for proposal submission.
- Issue the RPF.
- Conduct a preliminary evaluation to identify the respondents who will be invited to give on-site presentations.
- Schedule presentations. These may be open to all interested staff or limited to the RFP task group.
- Evaluate and score proposals and presentations.
- Make initial selection(s) and negotiate with preferred supplier(s).
- Award contract.

Because of the complexity of issuing an RFP and evaluating proposals, libraries should allow sufficient time for each phase. This is not a process that can be rushed.

Proposal evaluation and the selection procedure should be objective and demonstrate impartiality. All aspects of the process and proposals should be confidential. Evaluation of proposals is based on a balance of appropriateness of solution, vendor qualifications, vendor financial stability, price, and any other essential criteria defined by the library.

A less common method for securing information about possible content and service providers is the RFQ. The RFQ process is appropriate for com-

mon equipment or standard services where the specifications can easily identify the product or service and are less frequently used with e-content services
and suppliers. An RFQ may be used when discussions with bidders are not
required and when price is the main or only factor in selecting the successful
bidder. An RFQ also can be used to determine general price ranges prior to
issuing an RFP.

RFIs, RFPs, and RFQs require significant effort by the library and the companies that respond. Most often this work is undertaken when a new company
with attractive offerings enters the marketplace, the library is dissatisfied with a
current content and service provider, or an existing contract is about to expire.
RFPs are not appropriate when only one possible content supplier or service
provider can provide the content or services needed. Public agencies may
require the library to provide a sole-source justification if an RFP is not issued.

Focus Groups and Advisory Boards

Librarians have additional opportunities to foster communication with publishers, agents, vendors, aggregators, and other suppliers of content and services.
Many of these entities create focus groups and have standing advisory boards.
Focus groups are used for qualitative feedback on various areas such as general
evaluation of exiting products and advice on future directions, new product
development, and development of new sales models. These research groups are
formed as needed and disbanded when the intended purpose is fulfilled.

Advisory boards function in an ongoing, long-term capacity and provide
feedback to suppliers about their products, services, and business models.
Librarians have an opportunity to learn about new products and services,
provide feedback on existing products and services, and better understand
the information marketplace. Advisory boards offer a way for suppliers to
understand directly their customers' needs, wants, and expectations, and this
input can have a direct effect on product and service development. Fries and
James's survey of twelve information industry companies found that respondents considered advisory boards invaluable in their company's work.[3] Often
advisory boards are composed of members from specific client groups such
as community college librarians, public librarians, or K–12 school librarians
and media specialists.

Service as part of a focus group or on an advisory board should be
approached responsibly. Although one may be honored to be invited to serve
and may receive free meals and sometimes travel and housing support, it is
not a perk. Librarians should be careful not to hint that their participation

will result in additional business. Most discussions and demonstrations are to be treated confidentially. Focus groups and advisory boards have a serious purpose and provide an excellent venue for librarians to share their concerns and priorities.

Beta Testing

Another option to influence product and service development is for a library to be a beta tester. Beta testing involves testing a new product, software, service, or interface before it is released to the market. The purpose is to identify weak points, flaws, and problems so these can be corrected before general release. Working as a beta tester in the development of an automated system is more familiar to many librarians, but e-content and service providers also use beta sites to test their offerings.

Being a beta tester may generate a discounted price for the library, but it is often hard work. The library is serving as a collaborative development partner, and those involved in the testing should take their responsibilities seriously. The contribution of each partner must be meaningful and important. When a library agrees to be a beta site, a binding agreement is signed that spells out clear and formal expectations describing what the vendor and the library will contribute to the effort. This agreement usually includes a confidentiality waiver to protect the company. Being a beta tester can be extremely time-consuming and involve several people in various library units. If a library is willing and able to be a beta test site, the opportunity to influence the development of a new product or service can be both interesting and beneficial.

NEGOTIATION

Negotiating with publishers, vendors, subscription agents, and aggregators often seems like the most time-consuming aspect of relations with these e-content and service suppliers. Reaching agreement requires spending time in meetings, on the phone, and in e-mail exchanges. This can be stressful, especially when many contracts for e-content and with vendors and agents involve large amounts of money. Throughout this process, librarians should remember that both the supplier and the library are striving to represent their organizations effectively, that the supplier wants to sell products and services, and that the library wants to buy them. Negotiation is not necessarily adversarial, although it can become so. One should assume that both parties are bargaining in good faith until proven otherwise.

Librarians tend to think of negotiation primarily in relation to reaching agreement on the terms of a license for e-content (as introduced in chapter 4). Contracts for services with subscription agents and vendors are also negotiable and should be approached with the same attention to detail as when negotiating for content. Considerations that the library views as important should be clear from the onset and typically include specific performance expectations, such as the speed with which service questions are answered, quality of cataloging if provided, timeliness with which content is available, and frequency, format, and manner in which data are transferred between the content or service provider and the library. These data may be order confirmation records, cataloging records, or invoices. If the library is transferring business from one vendor or subscription agent to another, the contract usually specifies the assistance to be provided in the transition.

The library should ensure that the individuals with whom it is negotiating can speak for and negotiate on behalf of the company. Similarly, the library's representative should have comparable authority. Initial conversations may start with an individual selector or someone in the acquisitions or serials unit, but final negotiations often are the responsibility of a senior administrator in the library. Particularly complicated or contentious negotiation may involve attorneys representing the library or its parent organization.

People negotiate with each other every day about what to prepare for dinner (or the restaurant in which to eat), which plants to buy for the garden, and what appropriate bedtimes are for children on school nights and weekends. Librarians talk about negotiating reference questions. The ability to negotiate effectively is an essential skill. In their widely used book on negotiation and conflict resolution, *Getting to Yes,* Fisher and Ury stress what they call *principled negotiation.*[4] Principled negotiation, or negotiation on the merits, has four basic elements: separating the people from the problem; focusing on interests, not positions; inventing multiple options looking for mutual gains before deciding what to do; and insisting that the result be based on some objective standard.

The first element, separating one's emotional reaction to the participants from the negotiation underway, may be the most problematic. People have difficulty separating the problem to be resolved from the individuals sitting on the other side of the negotiation table, their feelings about those individuals, and perhaps the company they represent. They tend to hear what they think is being said, based on how they feel about the speaker. Actively and attentively listening and demonstrating that one understands are core skills in effective negotiation.

Focusing on interests, not positions, means avoiding going into the negotiations with a predetermined bottom line. Librarians should be able to separate position from interests. A librarian may state, "We refuse to renew our Big Deal agreement with publisher X and we need to terminate it." At a more basic level, the problem is "Our budget allocation has been reduced and we cannot afford the current cost of content," which is a need and thus, according to Fisher and Ury, the interest that should guide negotiation. Starting with interests instead of positions opens the door to effective negotiation by making clear the basic problem to be solved.

Once the library and the other party or parties at the negotiating table begin thinking in terms of problems, then they can begin thinking of alternative solutions. Librarians are often effective at brainstorming multiple creative options when solving problems or planning projects. They need to bring this open mindset to the negotiating table. Fisher and Ury observe that "skill at inventing options is one of the most useful assets a negotiator can have."[5] This is most effective when both parties agree to offer and consider various options and withhold judgment until all possible solutions have been considered.

The fourth basic element, insisting on using objective criteria, can be challenging when negotiating licenses and contracts. It is more feasible in some areas. When negotiating with an e-content provider for MARC records that will accompany the content, the library can reference accepted cataloging standards (e.g., catalog records that describe the e-content, not the print version) and proper placement of accurate linking data. This is more measurable than requiring "good" cataloging. Industry standards and government regulations (e.g., load-bearing standards for floors that will hold book stacks) and accepted valuation sources (e.g., Kelley Blue Book for vehicles) are not available for most of the e-content and services in which libraries are interested. Citing best practices for licenses, such as SERU (see chapter 4), may be helpful. One reason librarians are leery of nondisclosure clauses is that they prohibit sharing and comparing what libraries are paying for the same content. In the absence of fair and objective standards, one approach is to use fair and reasonable procedures for resolving the conflicting interest.

The library has leverage it can bring to negotiations. The most powerful is walking away from the negotiation. The library can decide not to purchase or license access from the supplier with which it is negotiating. In 2010 the University of California (UC) went further in its response to Nature Publishing Group's (NPG) proposed price increase "of unprecedented magnitude" in a letter stating that faculty would be asked to cease submitting papers and undertaking peer review for NPG journals, resign from all NPG editorial and advisory boards, and not advertise jobs in NPG journals.[6] This memo and subsequent public statements from UC and NPG attracted international attention as the library community watched to see how the dispute would be resolved. Two months later, a joint statement from NPG and UC announced:

> Our two organizations have agreed to work together in the coming months to address our mutual short- and long-term challenges, including an exploration of potential new approaches and evolving publishing models. We look forward to a successful planning and experimentation process that results in mutual agreement that serves all stakeholder groups—NPG, the UC libraries, and the scholar community, thus avoiding the need for the boycott that had been discussed at an earlier stage.[7]

In February 2012, UC released an update covering several points, which concluded, "Although we have not yet reached agreement on a model that would allow us to add new NPG journal titles, UC and NPG have agreed to maintain their existing license while discussions continue."[8] Few libraries have the combined power of the UC system, but many librarians were heartened to see the results of the UC refusal to agree to yet another price increase.

Refusing to accept a price increase or a proposal is not the only option. Remember that content providers want to maintain their customers and hope to increase their volume of business. Libraries can offer incentives. For example, a library might offer to consolidate more of its ordering with a subscription agent in exchange for a lower service fee or with a vendor for a deeper discount. Libraries may consider making prepayments or setting up deposit accounts with a supplier if the supplier is financially sound. Research has shown that libraries with larger budgets are able to negotiate larger discounts. A report from Primary Research Group found that 25.6 percent of vendors that supply video and audio to libraries are open to price negotiation and that some libraries negotiated as much as 60 percent off the initial price.[9] A librarian cannot determine if a content or service provider is willing to negotiate without asking.

If the relationship between the vendor and the librarian is fair-minded and they share an understanding that both are trying to do their best for their organizations, an amicable settlement often can be reached. The key is to engage in principled negotiation, remove personalities from the equation, and focus on a solution that addresses the interests of all parties.

ONGOING COMMUNICATION

Effective communication is a central ingredient in the ongoing relationship between a library and a content or service provider. As Harrell notes, "Communication between libraries, publishers, and vendors has never been more critical to supplying resources to library customers in a transparent and seamless manner from the view of the customers."[10] Effective service depends on effective communication. Service has always been important in the relationship between libraries and their suppliers. This is even more important with the shift from hard copy to electronic content in which tangible products seldom changes hands and service defines the nature of access to e-content.

Appropriate individuals in the library (usually representing collection development and management and technical services) should meet with company representatives at least annually to discuss new offerings, changes in what the library needs, and persistent service concerns. Often these conversations are twice a year or quarterly. Company representatives may have different titles such as local field representative, regional sale representative, account executive, or head of institutional sales. Their goal is to develop and support their company's relationship with the library and increase the amount of business the library does with their company. They should be knowledgeable about their company's products and services, the library's special needs, and any customization implemented by the library. These meetings may be used to renegotiate contracts, update approval plans, and order new products and services. Unresolved service issues also may be a topic for discussion, although these should be addressed as they occur with the company's customer service representative and not accumulated and presented at an annual meeting with the sales representative.

Most libraries are in contact with their vendors and subscription agents many times during the year on various topics. Sales representatives communicate information on new products, services, and features and publishers and formats added to their offerings. They often provide forecasts of price changes in books and journals for the coming year. These data can help library develop their budget and plan allocations. Sales representatives may share information about in-person and online training tools for library staff and new features of their online system.

Resolving Problems

The most critical topic of communication between content and service providers and the library is problem resolution. Vendors, publishers, agents, and aggregators should have knowledgeable customer service representatives available during peak times in different time zones with toll-free telephone numbers. The speed and efficiency with which the service representatives handle issues are critical to their effectiveness. They should respond to problems reported via e-mail, phone, or an online problem-reporting system in a timely manner. If the service representative cannot immediately solve the problem, he or she should notify the library contact that the problem is receiving attention and when it will be resolved.

The library also has responsibilities in problem reporting and resolution. Library staff members should monitor data from automated systems and reports from the content or service provider. They should follow up on problem reports from others in the library. They should review invoices for accuracy and appropriate fees, service charges, and discounts and track timeliness in all areas important to the library. All problems should be documented in writing and conveyed to the appropriate company representative so they can be addressed. Some libraries keep a log of problems, the date they were reported and to whom, and the date of resolution. The library should give the representative detailed information about problems and the opportunity to correct them. Possible problems are

- errors
- unannounced or lengthy downtime
- tardiness in loading content to the supplier's platform
- tardiness in filling orders
- overcharges
- cataloging records that do not meet specified criteria
- unexpected service charges
- unexpected or unexplained price increases
- inaccurate invoices
- order record files or invoices that cannot be loaded into the library's system
- inadequate problem resolution

A documented history of problems is essential when reviewing a contract for renewal or considering alternative suppliers and service agencies.

Reviewing the Relationship

In addition to monitoring performance on an ongoing basis, libraries should conduct periodic, systematic reviews of their content suppliers and service providers to ensure that the relationship is meeting the library's needs and expectations. Problems that are documented when they occur should be analyzed at least annually for types of problems, number and frequency of their occurrence, and speed with which they are resolved. If the library has specified performance criteria in the service agreement or license, library staff can compare actual performance to these specifications. Some categories of problems, such as slow responses to the library, slow payments to suppliers, increasing frequency of mistakes, downsizing, and high staff turnover, may indicate vendor or agent cash flow problems or company instability.

Responsibility for keeping track of a supplier's performance and ensuring that it meets the terms of the contract or license is often shared between collection development and technical services librarians in larger libraries. Regardless of who is involved in its writing, an internal report should be prepared that includes data on problems, any variations from expected performance specified in the contract or license, and a recommendation about renewing the current agreement or, if problems are sufficiently egregious, terminating the agreement for cause. Fair and equitable dealing requires that libraries track their own obligations to vendors and document that these have been met (or not), as well.

Changing subscription agents and content suppliers, when the latter is possible, requires significant staff time and energy and is not a trivial undertaking, but if a relationship is unsatisfactory and the library's investment is not justified, action should be taken. Giving the agent or supplier an opportunity to remedy the problems should be the first option explored. Failing to correct problems is justification for seeking an alternative. Good stewardship of a library's resources demands it.

Conducting Business

Effective ongoing relationships depend on appropriate behavior on the part of both librarians and corporate representatives. Both parties have obligations to ensure that the relationship runs smoothly and successfully. Sales representatives should schedule their visits. Librarians have no obligation to meet with representatives who do not make appointments. Sales representatives should provide full disclosure about products, services, and prices. They should supply written proposals and offers. Without complete and accurate information, librarians cannot make informed decisions. Sale representatives should understand libraries and the technical language of librarianship. More important, they should know and understand the library they are visiting. They should listen carefully to the librarians' needs and expectations. They should provide early and clear notification of planned price increases and of services outages. They should realize that not all visits result in sales and avoid pressuring librarians with offers that have time-limited availability. Sales representatives should try, to the extent they can, to be the ongoing sales contact for their company. Librarians prefer not to have to explain their situation to a new representative every few months.

Customer service representatives fill a different role—focusing on the day-to-day work of the company, meeting library needs, and solving problems. Library staff members seldom meet customer services representatives in person, relying instead on e-mail and phone to communicate. Ideally, the company provides a single point of contact (sometimes called an account service manager) for service issues, plus either the name of a substitute or a clear hand-off system. Libraries should expect prompt and courteous service. Information should be clear and helpful. Excellent companies have excellent service representatives because they know how important responsive service is to libraries.

Librarians also have obligations in ensuring a satisfactory relationship with sales and service representatives. Many of these behaviors parallel those expected from company agents. Courtesy and respect are the currency of business dealings.

ADVICE FOR EFFECTIVE
MEETINGS WITH SALES REPRESENTATIVES

Librarians should be
- Ready when sales representatives arrive for appointments. This means being available at the schedule time and prepared.
- Courteous. Librarians should be polite and respectful. This includes such basic behaviors as focusing one's total attention on the meeting and having calls held.
- Honest and straightforward. Being truthful goes a long way in building trust, which, in turn, facilitates effective negotiation.
- Principled and ethical. Operating from principles and in accordance with professional and institutional ethics puts a librarian in a position of strength.
- Objective and unbiased. Librarians should not bring preconceptions and biases to the meeting. This may be difficult—librarians share a great deal via e-mail, blogs, and in person. Reports of positive and negative encounters and outcomes should not set

expectations for any other individual's meetings.

- Unemotional. Once emotions enter into the conversation, objectivity is lost.
- Attentive. Listening carefully to what is being said and considering before responding open the door to exploring options.
- Cautious about making immediate commitments. A consideration period is a normal part of conducting business. Offers should not always be accepted the day they are presented. Reflecting and discussing with others in the library are responsible ways to steward library resources.
- Attentive to the possibility of conflict of interest and careful about accepting gifts and hospitality that might influence responsible decisions.

SUMMARY

Librarians and content and service providers have different goals. Librarians want to purchase or lease content and contract for services. Publishers, aggregators, vendors, and agents want customers for their products and services. To achieve these ends, the parties need to agree to work together to advance their mutual interests. Building and maintaining effective relationships are central to conducting business.

The first step for librarians is learning about the marketplace and options that can meet the library's needs. Information sources can be informal or formal. Formal sources of information include RFIs, RFPs, and RFQs. One value in creating these formal documents is the development of a clear set of specifications detailing the library's needs and performance expectations. Focus groups and advisory boards offer an opportunity to learn more about a company and its products and services and to influence their development. Serving as a beta tester for a new product or service also provides this opportunity.

The ability to negotiate effectively is important for librarians. Effective negotiation is principled and separates the people from the problem to be resolved; focuses on interests, not positions; explores multiple options before making the final decision; and, to the extent possible, measures results against an objective standard or best practice. Librarians should assume that all parties in the negotiation are acting in good faith until proven otherwise.

Successful ongoing communication is essential to sustain working relationships. Regular and frequent meetings with sales representatives and attention to problem reporting and resolution are recommended. Librarians have a responsibility to track and report problems as soon as they are identified. The ongoing relationship should be reviewed systematically at least annually. This involves comparing performance expectations and other obligations set out in the license or contract against actual performance during a determined time period. When performance is well documented, it can serve as the basis for contract renegotiation, renewal, or termination. Sustaining a successful business relationship requires that both librarians and corporation representatives act courteously and respectfully while being attentive to their obligations and responsibilities.

Suggested Readings

American Association of Law Libraries, "Guide to Fair Business Practices for Legal Publishers," Approved by the Executive Board Nov. 2002; 2nd. ed. approved July 2006; revised 2nd. ed. approved April 2008. www.aallnet.org/main-menu/Advocacy/Recommendedguidelines/fair-practice-guide.html.

Anderson, Rick. *Buying and Contracting for Resources and Services: A How-to-Do-It Manual for Librarians.* How-to-Do-It Manuals for Librarians 125. New York: Neal-Schuman, 2004.

Anderson Rick, Jane F. White, and David Burke. "How to Be a Good Customer: Building and Maintaining Productive Relationships with Vendors." *Serials Librarian* 48, no. 3/4 (June 2005): 322–23.

Ball, David. *Managing Suppliers and Partners for the Academic Library.* London: Facet, 2005.

Calvert, Philip, and Marion Read. "RFPs: A Necessary Evil or Indispensable Tool?" *Electronic Library* 24, no. 5 (2006): 649–61.

Coe, George. "Managing Customer Relationships: A Book Vendor Point-of-View." *Journal of Library Administration* 44, no. 3/4 (2006): 43–55.

Cole, Louise. "A Journey into E-resource Administration Hell." *Serials Librarian* 49, no. 1/2 (2005): 141–54.

Courtney, Keith. "Library/Vendor Relations: An Academic Publisher's Perspective." *Journal of Library Administration* 44, no. 3/4 (2006): 57–68.

De Jong, Mark. "Good Negotiations: Strategies for Negotiating Vendor Contracts." *Bottom Line: Managing Library Finances* 22, no. 2 (2009): 37–41.

Fries, James R., and John R. James. "Library Advisory Boards: A Survey of Current Practice among Selected Publishers and Vendors." *Journal of Library Administration* 44, no. 3/4 (2006): 85–93.

Gagnon, Ronald A. "Library/Vendor Relations from a Public Library Perspective." *Journal of Library Administration* 44, no. 3/4 (2006): 95–111.

Goodyear, Marilu, and Adrian W. Alexander. "Libraries as Customers: Achieving Continuous Improvement through Strategic Business Partnerships." *Library Acquisitions: Practice and Theory* 22, no. 1 (1998): 5–14.

Lam, Helen. "Library Acquisitions Management: Methods to Enhance Vendor Assessment and Library Performance." *Library Administration and Management* 18, no. 3 (Summer 2004): 146–54.

Morrisey, Locke J. "Ethical Issues in Collection Development." *Journal of Library Administration* 47, no. 3/4 (2008): 163–71.

Nalhotra, Deepak, and Max H. Bazerman. "Investigative Negotiation." *Harvard Business Review* 85, no. 9 (Sept. 2007): 72–78.

Percik, David. "Any Answers? Questions for Suppliers." *Legal Information Management* 11, no. 1 (2011): 2–9.

Raley, Sarah, and Jean Smith, "Community College Library/Vendor Relations: You Can't Always Get What You Want . . . or Can You?" *Journal of Library Administration* 44, no. 3/4 (2006): 187–202.

Staminson, Christine, Bob Persing, and Chris Beckett, presenters; Chris Brady, recorder. "What They Never Told You about Vendors in Library School." *Serials Librarian* 56, no. 1/4 (2009): 139–45.

Westfall, Micheline Brown. "Using a Request for Proposal (RFP) to Select a Serials Vendor: The University of Tennessee Experience." *Serials Review* 37, no. 2 (June 2011): 87–92.

Williams, Virginia Kay, and Kathy A. Downes. "Assessing Your Vendors' Viability." *Serials Librarian* 59, no. 3/4 (2010): 313–24.

Zhang, Sha Li, Dan Miller, and John Williams. "Allocating the Technology Dividend in Technical Services through Using Vendor Services." *Library Collections, Acquisitions, and Technical Services* 26, no. 4 (Winter 2002): 379–93.

Notes

1. One example that gives a flavor of The Digital Shift content is Michael Kelley, "A Guide to Publishers in the Library Ebook Market" (Feb. 24, 2012), *The Digital Shift*, www.thedigitalshift.com/2012/02/ebooks/a-guide-to-publishers-in-the-library-ebook-market.

2. Knut Dorn, "Sustaining Vision and Values for an International Subscription Agency: Harrassowitz," *Serials Review* 37, no. 4 (Dec. 2011): 241–318.

3. James R. Fries and John R. James, "Library Advisory Boards: A Survey of Current Practice among Selected Publishers and Vendors," *Journal of Library Administration* 44, no. 3/4 (2006): 85–93.

4. Roger Fisher and William Ury, with Bruce Patton, ed., *Getting to Yes: Negotiating Agreement without Giving In*, 3rd ed. (New York: Penguin, 2011).

5. Ibid., 58.

6. Laine Farley, Richard A. Scheider, and Brian E.C. Schottlaender, to UC Divisional Chairs and Members of the UC Faculty, "Informational Update on a Possible UC Systemwide Boycott of the Nature Publishing Group" (June 4, 2010), http://libraries.ucsd.edu/collections/Nature_Faculty_Letter-June_2010.pdf.

7. "Statement from the University of California and Nature Publishing Group" (Aug. 15, 2010), http://osc.universityofcalifornia.edu/npg/statement_092510.html.

8. Laine Farley et al., "University of California Update on Discussions with Nature Publishing Group" (Feb. 13, 2012), http://osc.universityofcalifornia.edu/npg/NPG_Statement_2012_02_13.pdf.

9. Primary Research Group, *Library Use of Video and Audio* (New York: Primary Research Group, 2011).

10. Jeanne Harrell, "Literature of Acquisitions in Review, 2008–9," *Library Resources and Technical Services* 56, no. 1 (Jan. 2012): 8.

CHAPTER 6

WORKING ACROSS ORGANIZATIONAL UNITS TO ACQUIRE AND MANAGE E-RESOURCES

THE DAY-TO-DAY OPERATION of managing e-resources is multifaceted, nonlinear, and often cross-departmental. Many of the operations are cyclical in nature in libraries. This is sometimes called life cycle management. Life cycle management begins with selection and advances to acquisition, cataloging, management, renewal or cancellation, and transfer to storage or withdrawal, with intermediate steps along the way. Managing the communication, handoffs, and interoperability is complex. Traditional workflows and divisions of responsibility are no longer effective or efficient when working with e-content, yet many librarians continue to try to tweak existing processes to make them fit. This chapter does not seek to define the best organizational approach or identify where responsibilities should be assigned. Instead, it describes these responsibilities to give librarians a deeper understanding of what they are, the decisions that need attention, and their interrelated complexity. To that end, this chapter provides an overview of the functional areas involved in managing e-resources, describes electronic resource management systems, considers approaches to description and access, and looks briefly at updating, maintaining, and deleting records, and responding to problems reported with e-content.

FUNCTIONAL AREAS

Managing e-resources through their life cycle encompasses many tasks that parallel those for managing other types of content, but it differs in significant ways because of the nature of e-content. More library departments and staff members are usually involved. For example, individuals with subject selection responsibility, collection development managers, and acquisitions staff may be in contact with a content provider during a trial and as the license and price are negotiated. Library automated systems staff may be involved in the consideration of technological issues even before the selection decision is made and then in supporting discovery and access through the e-content life cycle. The management and delivery of e-content depend on distributed yet related responsibilities in both the library and many interconnected library and vendor systems. Some libraries have created new units that pull together all staff members who are involved in the e-content life cycle.[1] Others rely on a matrix-based team that informally unites the individuals who have various related duties.[2] Ensuring that the necessary staff members know when to perform their responsibilities requires coordination and constant communication.

Placing an order for e-content does not result in delivery of a physical item that is receipted and then passed on for cataloging. Libraries rely on the supplier to notify them that access to a title has been activated. If the content supplier is unable or unwilling to provide access notification, the library must check for access on a routine basis. The library also relies on the supplier to provide an appropriate URL for accessing the title. At the point that access has been activated on the supplier's platform, the library then can move to setting up services that authenticate and authorize users and to providing intellectual access through its online public access catalog, A–Z lists, and subject guides. Local practice determines which of the options to facilitate discovery and access are selected.

The following flowchart (fig. 6.1) illustrates a simplified workflow for selecting, ordering, and making an e-resource (in this case, an e-journal or database) available for users. Imbedded in this process are many responsibilities, including these:

- managing trials to evaluate content and interfaces
- negotiating licenses
- registering a title for access
- overseeing a proxy server
- implementing and maintaining linking services
- maintaining a knowledge base
- providing intellectual access through the means selected by the library

Each library must decide where such tasks reside within its organization. The sample workflow makes clear the need for effective communication to ensure that each task is accomplished when appropriate.

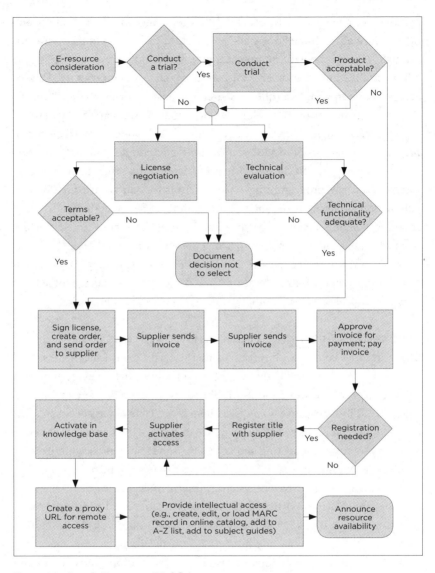

Figure 6.1   Sample E-resources Workflow

Registration is one example of how processes have become more complex when e-content is involved. In the paper environment, a customer number usually appeared on the mailing label. Now that number is sent via e-mail or in a paper confirmation of payment. This number may be required as one step in the process of activating institutional access to an e-journal. A library staff member must go to the publisher's or supplier's website and enter the customer number to access the site on which to enter pertinent administrative data—a user name and password, the IP address range for the institution, and other information. If the library adds or deletes IP addresses in the future, for example, it must know the appropriate user name and password to access the administrative information area and effect the change. Libraries need a reliable, accurate mechanism (often a shared spreadsheet or database) to record the unique customer number, along with the related user name and password.

Another example of complex and multifaceted work is that required to manage large batches of MARC records for e-content. Respondents to a survey by Mugridge and Edmunds identified numerous tasks, including customizing records, programming, writing scripts for data transformation and automation, adapting load tables to accommodate new record sets, troubleshooting, deleting records in batches, and writing FTP scripts to retrieve files from providers and load them into a local server for manipulation.[3]

Much of the needed expertise may be resident in the library's information technology or automated systems unit, but some libraries manage these tasks within technical services. In others, staff across a library share tasks.

ELECTRONIC RESOURCE MANAGEMENT SYSTEMS

The increasing volume of e-resources that libraries collect has necessitated an effective way to record and track the complex information associated with pricing, licenses, permitted and prohibited uses, scope of the content, and more. In addition, because no physical item is available to pass between units or individuals, libraries need an alternative to manage the numerous handoffs necessary to make discovering and accessing these materials easy for users.

Libraries with a limited number of e-resources may be able to manage e-resources in a paper-based system, filing printed copies of the licenses alphabetically, using existing acquisitions procedures to place and track orders, and recording key information on spreadsheets. Typical information recorded is title of resource and licensor, license details and terms of use, purchase order number, cost, authentication and registration information, and renewal date. This approach can be sufficient when a library acquires or leases access to a modest number of e-resources.

Using paper files is no longer sufficient in many libraries because of the volume of e-resources they manage. One solution is an electronic sources management (ERM) system, which stores data that the current ILS generation was not built to include. Initially developed by libraries in-house to handle e-journal subscriptions and their licenses, ERM systems now are available commercially and also manage e-book and e-journal packages. Some ERM systems interact with the ILS so that libraries can avoid duplicating acquisitions activities (ordering, budgeting, and fund accounting). Ideally, an ERM system accommodates all processes and interacts with all tools used to manage e-resources and serves as one point of maintenance and business intelligence by pulling together the information needed to perform various functions. These include acquisitions, public display, license management, collection evaluation, reporting, and statistical analysis. ERM systems send alerts about the next task to be performed. A survey of academic librarians in 2011 identified their top six ERM priorities as workflow management, license management, statistics management, administrative information storage, acquisitions functionality, and interoperability.[4] A more detailed list of specific functions an ERM system can be expected to perform are as follows:

- Accommodate comprehensive acquisitions information (purchase order number, price, start and end dates for the subscription period, vendor name, vendor ID, fund or budget code, invoice number and date, and renewal date).
- Generate an alert when renewal date approaches.
- Integrate with the ILS acquisitions module (including use of vendor lists/tables) and the institution's finance system.
- Track selection decisions (e.g., decision to not purchase).
- Support authentication and registration.
- Record technical and administrative contacts.
- Manage trials.
- Manage licenses (record license details and terms of use; display selected usage rights to users).
- Support recording of multiple titles supplied through one license.
- Be able to attach an e-resource to an existing license and an addendum to an existing license.
- Comply with appropriate standards.
- Provide local link resolvers with appropriate data.
- Create brief catalog records and facilitate MARC record management.
- Support public display features (A–Z e-journal list, A–Z database list, library subject pages, etc.) with appropriate metadata.
- Identify technical requirements.
- Import, store, and export usage data in a usable form.
- Generate preprogrammed and custom reports.
- Manage queues for distributing tasks and send alerts to push tasks.

The need for ERM system standards prompted the Digital Library Federation (www.diglib.org) to create the Electronic Resource Management Initiative (ERMI) in 2002. Its purpose was to develop a list of functional requirement for an ERM system, identify data elements and common definitions for consistency, provide potential schemas, and identify and support data standards.[5] Most commercial vendors providing ERM systems follow these standards. ERMI was followed by ERMI 2, which revised the data dictionary and sought to incorporate standardized licensing terms. The National Information Standards Organization's ERM Data Standards and Best Practices Project is a successor to ERMI and ERMI 2. NISO's 2012 *Making Good on the Promise of ERM: A Standards and Best Practices Discussion Paper* analyzes and evaluates the current state of standards and best practices that can be applied to ERM systems.[6]

An international initiative building on the ERMI work is EDItEUR's ONIX for Publication Licenses (ONIX-PL), "an XML format for the communication of license terms for digital publications in a structured and substantially encoded form, designed to serve the interests of all parties in the licensing chain."[7] ONIX-PL aims to solve the problem of consistently recording licensing information in ERM systems, but it has not been widely implemented.

Another standard that facilitates a successful ERM system has been developed by COUNTER. This standard defines specific data gathering, access and usage tracking, terminology, processing of usage data, and standards for report layout, format, and delivery. A vendor that is COUNTER-compliant supplies data about a given e-resource in a format that can be used by a COUNTER-compliant ERM systems to harvest usage statistics for analysis and comparison.

ERM systems must be populated with the necessary information, which can be labor- and time-intensive. Options include batch loading MARC records extracted from the ILS, manually inputting data, and populating with data from a knowledge base of information about the titles a library owns or has the rights to access. ERM system vendors may enhance the ERM data with supplemental resources and bibliographic and holdings records, as well as contact information and, in some cases, license information. Inevitably, library staff members have to add additional records and complete license information.

Library system vendors, subscription agents, and third-party companies offer ERM systems. These ERM system providers link and manage a given library's subscriptions through OpenURL link resolvers and, often, A–Z listing services. If a library uses several tools from the same company, a knowledge base can be shared across them. One potential problem with ERM systems from third parties is the extent to which they integrate with a library's ILS and with other third-party tools. ERM systems from systems vendors and third parties may be cost-prohibitive for some libraries. Many subscription agents also offer ERM services that may or may not integrate with a library's existing tools and systems. Use of ERM services offered by subscription agents depends on a library's use of these companies' subscription services. If such a service is used, the library should ensure that the data in a third party's ERM can be exported for future migration to other systems. Another option is an open-source ERM system developed by one library and made available free of charge to others.

Libraries often distribute e-resource management responsibilities over several departments, even when they use an ERM system. Depending on the type and size of the library, units or staff responsible for cataloging, acquisitions, serials, collection management, systems and information technology, library administration, and reference may be involved. An ERM system that facilitates communication through task queuing and automatic handoffs can help avoid fragmented workflow and assist in making e-resources quickly and easily discoverable and accessible by users.

Knowledge Bases and OpenURL Linking

Because many ERM and web-scale discovery systems depend on the accuracy and currency of a knowledge base (also known as a resource list in web-scale discovery), a complete and reliable knowledge base is essential. Knowledge bases are central to the process of OpenURL linking because they record the universe of resources available, where content is, and which versions of specific objects a particular library's users are entitled to access. Using the knowledge base, an OpenURL link resolver determines if an item (article, book, etc.) is available electronically and what the appropriate copy is for a user. The link resolver extracts information received in an OpenURL and uses the knowledge base to augment and correct the data, find services available to a specific user for a specific item, and create a link to the desired item. OpenURL linking reduces the number of dead links and can increase use of the library's licensed content by improving it visibility. OpenURL knowledge bases usually have a close relationship with ERM systems because the link resolver and the ERM system use the same metadata. Link resolvers and their associated knowledge bases are usually positioned as part of a company's suite of products and are rarely offered as stand-alone products.[8]

Content hosts and full-text databases deliver holdings information and some-times MARC records to knowledge base developers to inform those systems about the extent of content on the delivery platform. Some knowledge base services then send holdings data to institutional A–Z lists and link resolvers and send MARC records to the library for the library's online public access catalog. In these cases, the library must supply its knowledge base developer with its holdings details. The quality of a knowledge base depends on data that content providers send to the knowledge base developer. To address this, the international community has developed *KBART: Knowledge Bases and Related Tools,* a recommended practice to guide content providers in preparing their title lists, which populate knowledge bases.[9] These guidelines define the metadata structure and data guidelines for use by all in the information supply chain. Another initiative growing on collaborative work is Improving OpenURLs through Analytics (IOTA) (www.openurlquality .org), which makes use of log files from institutions and vendors to analyze ele-ment frequency and patterns contained within OpenURL strings. The resulting reports inform vendors about where to make improvements to their OpenURL strings so that OpenURL requests resolve to a correct record.

Individual libraries do not need to maintain detailed information about the materials in each of their subscription packages locally. They can rely instead on knowledge bases maintained on behalf of a broader library community. ILS ven-dors, subscription agents, and service providers offer knowledge bases for a fee. These are customized to the library, reflecting the library's titles and holdings or coverage. A knowledge base updates URLs, movement of titles within databases and packages, and publisher information.

DISCOVERY AND ACCESS

A core responsibility of libraries is to support their users' discovery of and access to their collections, whether on-site, in storage, or remotely accessed. The traditional way to support discovery and access is to add descriptive records to a catalog, generally to an online public access catalog, where records are in MARC format. Some libraries had and many continue to have separate catalogs or finding tools for different categories of content, for example, media, micro-forms, rare books, archives, and government documents. Over time, however, many libraries abandoned these separate lists and incorporated these materials into their catalogs to simplify the user discovery experience.

As libraries have added e-content to their collections, they often have taken several approaches to support discovery and access, including separate files or lists. They may use one or more of the following:

- MARC records in the local catalog with links to the content
- A–Z list for e-journals with links to the content
- A–Z list for databases with links to the content
- subject lists for databases and e-book packages with links to the content
- links from subject and class guides

This array of possibilities offers several options for users, but it adds complexity and can create confusion. Assuring timely, accurate, and comprehensive access through so many channels requires redundant URL and holdings updates to multiple places, which can be a significant workload on staff. An ERM system and a current and comprehensive knowledge base can facilitate some of this work.

Deciding how to support discovery of and access to e-content is a local library decision. Crum identifies the issues to consider in making decisions about the type of discovery to provide users as "usability, staff time, local control, standards and interoperability, and flexibility."[10] Balancing these issues depends on staffing availability, financial resources, local user community needs and preferences, and available technology.

Libraries do have choices about where to facilitate discovery and access. Although librarians traditionally view the catalog as the authoritative and comprehensive source for discovery and access information, libraries might consider how often users discover, for example, e-journal content or U.S. government documents through the public catalog. In most cases, users start with an A–Z list to locate a journal title or identify and link to a full-text article through an index, database, or web search engine.[11] This suggests that creation of catalog records for some types of e-content could be abandoned in some libraries in favor of other access paths, eliminating both confusion and maintenance work. Before taking this step, libraries should conduct user research to determine how users search for and link to e-resources and focus on the paths most used by their user community. Libraries also should ensure that a different approach does not create problems elsewhere in the e-content life cycle.

One potential problem for user access when e-journals are not reflected in the catalog is split holdings in which more recent years are available electronically and older volumes are available in print. One solution is to provide a persistent message on an A–Z list page alerting users that print holdings are recorded in the catalog. Larger libraries often purchase extensive or complete retrospective e-holdings, which mitigates this problem.

Another consideration is that the ILS often serves as the audit trail for financial transactions. In this case, at least a brief record for these titles is needed in the library system, whether is displays to the public or not, to track payment. An additional difficulty may arise if the ILS is the source for bibliographic data that is displayed through the A–Z list, e-journal finder, or other e-resource-specific finding aid. In some cases, these external tools are refreshed periodically using data maintained in the catalog. Conversely, the source of data that updates records in the catalog, A–Z lists, and other finding aids may come from a knowledge base provided by an ILS vendor or other third parties. This means that the source data must have appropriate fields against which to match, which necessitates creating entries that facilitate this action. Understanding how catalog records interact with ERM systems, link resolvers, knowledge bases, and finding tools is essential before making policy decisions about where and how to record data.

Some libraries create subject lists and other discovery tools that generally operate outside the standard processes that update catalog records and A–Z lists. Many academic libraries expect their subject specialists and subject liaisons to keep these additional lists and discovery tools current, a task that is often a lower priority. Manually maintained guides often get stale and can misguide users. Libraries should carefully consider the effort necessary to keep these tools current compared to their value as a means of discovery.

Local Cataloging

Cataloging e-resources presents numerous challenges, which became apparent when libraries began adding e-journals while retaining print versions of the same title. The first decision was whether to create a new record for the e-version or to add it to the record for the print version. The latter approach was appealing for three reasons: librarians had been using this method to add microform holdings to records for print journal; it is easier and quicker for catalogers; and it collocates equivalent works in different formats, making discovery easier for the user. This is called the multiple version (often called mulver) or single record approach. Catalogers would indicate the availability of an electronic version by adding a MARC 856 field (information needed to locate and access an electronic resource) to the existing record for the print. This approach is logical, but it often creates problems later in the e-resources life cycle.

When catalogers realized that the e-versions of journals often were not exactly the same as the print, carried a different ISSN, or had a different name, many began to create separate records to describe the e-version correctly. The Cooperative Online Serials Program (CONSER) of the Program for Cooperative Cataloging, recognizing legitimate reasons for combining versions on a single record, approved both the single record and separate record model in 1994.[12] A noted above, another reason for creating separate records is the need to match incoming data (maintenance-level records, URL updates, withdrawals from aggregator packages) with existing catalog records. If the versions are reflected in separate catalog records, incoming data can be programmed to behave in predictable ways. Theoretically, the public catalog display can be designed to merge records to improve the user experience. Many libraries have decided that combining data for different versions (print and electronic) in a single record presents too many difficulties for maintenance over time.

Another cataloging challenge arose when multiple e-content suppliers began offering the same serial. Many libraries have access to the same title in several ways (e.g., from publishers, from aggregators). The problem is compounded by aggregators buying one another and publishers pulling titles from an aggregation. Although libraries have generally abandoned the single record approach, they are not interested in several records for the same content provided by numerous suppliers. To address this, CONSER implemented the provider-neutral record policy in 2003 for serials.[13] A provider-neutral record is separate from that for the print versions and covers all versions of the same online serial in one record. In 2009 the Program for Cooperative Cataloging's Monographic Bibliographic Record Program (BIBCO) implemented a provider-neutral record policy for monographs.[14] Provider-neutral records support repeatable MARC 856 fields (Electronic Location and Access) to record the URLs for access from various providers. These records are adaptable to local access methods that use record sets, ERM systems, OpenURL resolvers and knowledge bases, databases that provide full text or citations to content, and third-party services. Libraries increasingly use provider-neutral records.

The growing number of packages with hundreds and often thousands of e-titles to which libraries now provide access has made cataloging each e-title locally impossible. Libraries, however, continue to want to add records, particularly for e-books, to their catalogs. Evidence indicates that online public access catalogs remain users' preferred way of accessing e-books, especially within academic libraries.[15] Adding records for e-books to the catalog increases their use.[16] A 2011 Primary Research Group study found that 85.1 percent of the e-books in academic libraries and 38 percent in public libraries were represented by MARC records in their catalogs.[17] This likely reflects a frequent public library practice of using e-book aggregators' platforms for discovery instead of their local catalogs. The frequency with which libraries provided MARC records for downloadable video and audio was similar. Libraries had MARC records in their catalogs for 62.3 percent of their downloadable video and audio and 55.2 percent of videos available in streamed format.[18] Large research libraries that add, for example, 100,000 items per year to their catalogs may catalog less than 30 percent locally.[19]

Batch Loading Records

Libraries have turned to loading batches of records provided by publishers, aggregators and other content suppliers, subscription agents, and service providers. Some e-content suppliers provide free records with their bundled content, and some charge for them. Primary Research Group found that 55.8 percent of libraries that had MARC records for their e-books had records provided by e-book publishers or vendors.[20] E-books aggregators such as OverDrive and 3M's Cloud Library will provide MARC records, but delivery of the records to a library may lag behind when a book is made available for a library's patron's use. Serials agents and service providers often provide, for a fee, monthly feeds of MARC records for e-journals regardless of vendor or where the content is hosted, offering either a full title file or records only for new, changed, or deleted records.

The quality of e-book records available from providers varies considerably. These records may consist of only basic bibliographic information such as author, title, and ISBN (which might be incorrectly transcribed from the print version), along with the URL pointing to the title. Other records may be more complete and may conform to the Program for Cooperative Cataloging guidelines for creating provider-neutral catalog records. Records provided by book vendors tend to be better records than those provided by publishers and aggregators because book vendors are familiar with library expectations and have been providing high-quality records for many years as part of their shelf-ready programs. Subscription services that provide records for U.S. federal documents (97 percent of which are available electronically) have an equally long history of providing records that meet most libraries' quality expectations.[21]

The understanding of what is meant by high-quality cataloging records provided for batch loading varies. Luther explains, "The quality of metadata is best measured by its effectiveness in supporting the goals of the stakeholders to ensure book discovery."[22] Further, good catalog records are consistent from record to record and file to file, have complete core elements, meet an agreed-on standard, and are distributed in a timely manner. Martin and Mundle examined records for e-books from one publisher and identified three types of problems: access issues, load issues, and what they called record-quality issues. They explained these as "access issues prevented users from accessing the e-book, load issues prevented the records from being loaded into the catalog, and record-quality issues hampered users' ability to locate the records in the catalog or presented confusing information."[23] The first two are critical problems. Records with missing or incomplete links are worth very little to the user. If the library cannot load the batch, even those records that have valid links are inaccessible. Another serious problem is the ability to match records from multiple suppliers and avoid duplicate records for the same title in the catalog. Libraries are still working to implement provider-neutral records when batch loading records from a variety of sources.

Record quality (the extent to which records align with local and national descriptive practices) can be less critical, but still frustrating for libraries and their catalogers who value such elements as consistent series treatment, extensive description, several subject headings, and added entries for individuals of local importance. Batch loading records necessitates a compromise between quality and quantity. Libraries rarely can afford to catalog all e-content titles locally in a timely manner, yet they pay considerable sums for the content and need to make it accessible to users. Local cataloging policies and practices often must change to accept "good enough" records. Several libraries edit the vendor-supplied records in batch mode, aiming to catch and fix the most egregious problems that prevent discovery and access. A frequently used tool is MarcEdit, a free customizable MARC editing utility, developed and maintained by Terry Reese.[24] ILSs that search key words and offer sophisticated indexing may compensate records shortcomings.

Preliminary checking of records to be batch-loaded is important. It identifies another potential problem with records batches—their completeness, or match between the number of records and the number of titles in the package purchased. This can be determined by comparing these two numbers. If a package consists of 240 titles, the batch should contain 240 records. Another preliminary check is to establish that the records are in the agreed on format. Software can do much of the preliminary checking. Some libraries load records into a test catalog where they can be spot-checked by staff members, who may be systems staff, catalogers, or librarians with selection and public service responsibilities. This review can identify data elements that the library wishes to edit with a utility such as MarcEdit. Once records are checked and edited, they can be loaded into the ILS.

Batch loading may be the responsibility of automated systems staff, acquisition staff, cataloging staff, an e-resources librarian, another group or individual, or a combination of these. How the work is done and who does it is a local library decision. An important consideration is the speed with which this is done, on which the quality of access for library users depends.

A–Z Lists

Libraries began using static A–Z lists to facilitate access for users who wanted to limit their searches to e-content. These began as lists for e-journals and databases and were easy to maintain when lists were small. Information provided was usually the title, a link to the resources, and perhaps a brief description. As the number of titles has increased, maintaining these lists locally has become more labor-intensive and complicated. Aggregators' bundles with fluctuating titles have exacerbated the difficulty of keeping A–Z lists current and accurate. Some libraries also maintain A–Z lists of e-book packages.

The level of detail provided in A–Z lists varies. Lists maintained locally are, by necessity, less detailed. Ideally, all A–Z lists should do the following:

- Describe the content, including holdings.
- Explain any plug-in software required.
- List number of simultaneous users supported.
- Inform users if printing is permitted and, if it is, the extent permissible.
- Inform users if downloading is permitted and, if it is, the extent permissible.
- Explain how the content is viewable, e.g., PC, iPad, Kindle, Nook.
- Provide a link to additional information.

The only practical way for libraries to provide this level of information accurately for lengthy lists of journals and databases is to outsource to a third party. The library reports the databases and e-journals to which it subscribes, and the third party creates and dynamically maintains A–Z lists, using a knowledge base and incorporating institution-specific holdings. The choice of an A–Z list service provider relates to the decision about purchasing a link resolver product, which in turn affects the choice of a MARC record service. All should be interoperable. Librarians should assess the interoperability of these tools with each other and with their ILS and ERM system.

Updating, Maintaining, and Deleting Records

Keeping records in catalogs and A–Z lists accurate and current is a persistent responsibility. Many ERM systems offered by ILS vendors and other third parties provide options for batch loading holdings. This is useful when libraries purchase backfiles, but it means that the library must notify the service provider of any additions. Services that provide monthly MARC record loads generally offer the option of full title files or files that consist of records only for new, changed, or deleted records. Libraries must ensure that a mechanism correctly overlays records if data are changed or accurately deletes the proper record if the e-content is no longer available. Ensuring that changes are made in all locations (e.g., online catalog, A–Z lists, subject lists, subject and class guides) that direct library users to e-content requires careful and thorough attention. Some of this work can be automated with the help of third parties, but no library can assume that updating, maintaining, and deleting records can proceed without some level of human intervention.

Large groups of records may need to be deleted because, for example, a license has not been renewed and access to the content is terminated, or the library decides that a portion of records loaded for PDA should be removed because they are no longer timely. Staff members remove large blocks of records through batch deleting. Care must be taken so that only exactly those records to be removed from the catalog are actually deleted.

Next-Generation Catalogs and Web-Scale Discovery Solutions

Several libraries have implemented what are called next-generation catalogs.[25] Examples are Endeca, AquaBrowser (from Medialab Solutions), WorldCatLocal (from OCLC), and Primo (from Ex Libris). These offer increased functionality with intuitive user interfaces similar to popular websites. Next-generation catalogs are technically a discovery layer and not a traditional catalog, which draws only from local catalog records resident in the ILS. Next-generation catalogs harvest records from locally hosted library information silos, such as the ILS and digital repositories, and from remote databases and journals. Collective results are provided in a single interface. One goal of next-generation catalogs is to combine discovery and delivery efficiencies from both local and remote resources. In addition, next-generation catalogs have search engines that are better at ranking results by relevancy and usually offer faceted navigation that can narrow the search results.

Within the past few years, several web-scale management and discovery solutions have entered the library market. Examples are Serials Solutions Summon, EBSCO Discovery Services, Encore (from Innovative Interfaces), and Alma (from Ex Libris).These offerings aim to provide a single unified solution that streamlines routine tasks, including acquisitions, e-resource management, cataloging, and circulation. Perhaps more important, web-scale discovery services point users at a single, unified, comprehensive index of traditional library catalog records and article-level content almost instantaneously. The limitation is the amount of content that each web-scale discovery system contains, and all service providers are constantly adding additional content. Libraries using the same web-scale management solution share infrastructure costs and resources in the "cloud" and are able to collaborate in ways that are not restricted by local hardware and software. This shift to a consolidated collaborative environment requires greater attention to interoperability and compatibility of descriptive data or internal agreement to relinquish the need to control that data to gain the benefits expected. Breeding observes, "Libraries with significant investments in electronic content—which includes almost any academic library—are likely to be in the market for a discovery service if they do not already have one."[26] Until these solutions are widely adopted, most libraries will continue to work with a combination of ERM systems, knowledge bases, local catalogs, and link resolvers.

RESPONDING TO E-CONTENT PROBLEMS

The most frequent problem with e-content is inability to access a desired resource. Access problems can be reported by users or library employees. A user might simply report, "X is not working." The challenge is determining the cause, which can range from a broken link to issues on the supplier side (vendor, publisher, aggregator, etc.) to user error to the user bumping against the maximum number of simultaneous users permitted. The problem could be due to something as simple as an unpaid invoice or scheduled downtime. It can be as complex as the vendor moving content to different servers and not realizing that changing the domain name required the library to modify the proxy configuration entry for the resource. Troubleshooting can be a complex process and involve several people, including a subject specialist, a reference librarian, an e-resources librarian (if the library has one), serials or acquisitions staff, the vendor, library systems staff, and perhaps information technology staff who have oversight of the campus, school district, or other parent entity network.

The complexity of troubleshooting and the number of people that may be involved make clear that a process to manage problem reports, handoffs, and resolution tracking is critical. An effective process ensures that action is taken quickly, the person reporting the problem is notified when it is solved, and any persistent pattern of problems is documented. Some libraries use problem logs or trouble ticket systems. A web-based system allows people to submit problem reports using a form and automatically notifies the unit or individual responsible for researching and solving them. Many such systems record entries in an online problem log that can be updated as the problem is addressed and at the same time manage handoffs in the library. Some libraries use a simple e-mail system through which all problems are directed to the person responsible for resolution. Ideally, responsibility for monitoring the reports is assigned to one individual, who is able to resolve most of the problems and authorized to assign them to others as appropriate. Backup must be in place during absences.

Another type of problem that libraries may have to address is the result of a license breach, often some form of misuse or abuse such as systematic downloading of an entire journal issue or hundreds of articles at one time. The vendor usually shuts off access for the offending user's IP address, but it may shut off all access. When the vendor determines that a breach has occurred, it notifies the designated library staff member. The library and perhaps the larger unit in the parent organization with network responsibility must contact the offending user to explain the situation and get the user to cease the breaching activity. If the offender cannot be identified, the library may implement technological measures to control the type of misuse reported. When these steps are taken, the designated library employee contacts the vendor with assurance that the offending user will comply with the license or that the library has taken appropriate steps to prevent such misuse in the future. If the situation is not resolved promptly by a timeline usually set in the license, the vendor may be within its contractual rights to terminate all access. Thus, dealing with notifications of license breaches effectively and promptly is important.

SUMMARY

Managing the life cycle of e-content is complex and nonlinear, usually involving staff from various units within a library. Without a physical item in hand to pass to the next person, workflow must be managed virtually so that each unit or individual knows when the next step needs attention. ERM systems are one means to organize and control the vast amount of information needed to handle e-content over its life cycle and to manage workflow. Knowledge bases and link resolvers support accurate ERM information and facilitate linking to the e-content to which the library has access.

Libraries have choices about how they support discovery of their e-content. Frequently used means are records in the online catalog, A–Z lists, subject lists, and links from subject and class guides. Keeping these tools current presents constant challenges. Not all tools may be appropriate for all e-content. Libraries that acquire large packages of titles usually batch-load records for packages of titles into their catalogs. These records, created by content suppliers, frequently do not meet the quality standards libraries apply to in-house cataloging. Libraries make decisions about the most important elements supporting discovery and access and often compromise on some areas determined to be less essential. Many libraries use batch-editing software to correct problems and customize records to the extent considered important. Updating, maintaining, and deleting records are more complex tasks in the digital environment. Ideally, libraries rely on automated processes to address these responsibilities.

Problems with e-content can divided into two types—failure to access the content, and patron misuse that breaches the applicable license. Resolving the former may involve extensive troubleshooting and various library staff members. Ensuring that the problem is resolved quickly and the patron notified is important to keep patrons satisfied. Stopping patron abuse must be addressed equally quickly to ensure that the library and its users have continuing access to the resource in question.

No single model has emerged as the best way to manage the workflow and life cycle of e-content. Each library must decide how to do this in the context of its current organizational structure, location of expertise, and number of available staff.

Suggested Readings

Blackburn, Jonathan, and Sylvia A. Lowden. "Not for the Faint of Heart! A New Approach to Serials Management." *Serials Librarian* 60, no. 1/4 (2011): 61–74.

Breeding, Marshall. "Helping You Buy Electronic Resource Management Systems." *Computers in Libraries* 28, no. 7 (2008): 6–96.

———. *Next-Gen Library Catalogs*. Tech Set 1. New York: Neal-Schuman, 2010.

Chen, Xiatian, and Stephen Wynn. "E-journal Cataloging in an Age of Alternatives: A Survey of Academic Libraries." *Serials Librarian* 57, no. 1/2 (2009): 96–110.

Chew, Chiat Naun. "Next Generation OPACS: A Cataloging Viewpoint." *Cataloging and Classification Quarterly* 48, no. 4 (2010): 330–42.

Collins, Maria D. D. "ERM Systems: Background, Selection, and Implementation." In *Managing the Transition from Print to Electronic Journals and Resources: A Guide for Library and Information Professionals,* ed. Maria D. D. Collins and Patrick L. Carr, 181–206. New York: Routledge, 2008.

———. "Staffing Trends and Issues in E-resources Management." In *Managing the Transition from Print to Electronic Journals and Resources: A Guide for Library and Information Professionals,* ed. Maria D. D. Collins and Patrick L. Carr, 109–28. New York: Routledge, 2008.

De Fino, Melissa, and Mei Ling Lo. "New Roads for Patron-Driven E-books: Collection Development and Technical Services Implications of a Patron-Driven Acquisitions Pilot at Rutgers." *Journal of Electronic Resources Librarianship* 23, no. 4 (2011): 327–38.

Grogg, Jill E. "Using a Subscription Agent for E-journal Management." *Journal of Electronic Resources Librarianship* 22, no. 1/2 (2010): 7–10.

Harnett, Eric, et al. "Opening a Can of wERMS: Texas A&M University's Experiences in Implementing Two Electronic Resources Management Systems." *Journal of Electronic Resources Librarianship* 22, no. 1/2 (2010): 18–27.

Hepfer, Cindy, Susan Davis, and Daisy P. Waters. "Transforming Technical Services Units to Accommodate Electronic Resource Management." In *Perspectives on Serials in the Hybrid Environment,* ed. Harriet Lightman and John P. Blosser, 18–36. Chicago: American Library Association, 2007.

Kasprowski, Rafal. "Best Practice and Standardization Initiatives for Managing Electronic Resources." *Bulletin of the American Society for Information Science and Technology* 35, no. 1 (Oct./Nov. 2008): 13–19.

Lowe, M. Sara. "Clear as Glass: A Combined List of Print and Electronic Journals in the Knowledge Base." *Journal of Electronic Resources Librarianship* 20, no. 3 (2008): 169–77.

Luther, Judy. *Streamlining Book Metadata Workflow.* White paper prepared for the National Information Standards Organization and OCLC Online Computer Library Center, Inc. Baltimore: NISO; Dublin, OH: OCLC, 2009. www.niso.org/publications/white_papers/StreamlineBookMetadataWorkflowWhitePaper.pdf.

Mugridge, Rebecca L., and Jeff Edmunds. "Using Batchloading to Improve Access to Electronic and Microform Collections." *Library Resources and Technical Services* 53, no. 1 (Jan. 2009): 53–61.

Pennell, Charley. "The Role of the Online Catalog as an E-resource Access and Management Tool." In *Managing the Transition from Print to Electronic Journals and Resources: A Guide for Library and Information Professionals,* ed. Maria D. D. Collins and Patrick L. Carr, 167–79. New York: Routledge, 2008.

Shroyer, Andrew. "Your Input Sought . . . Streamlining Registration and Cataloging? . . . Return to Print?" *Serials Librarian* 61, no. 3/4 (2011): 346–52.

Stachokas, George. "Electronic Resources and Mission Creep: Reorganizing the Library for the Twenty-First Century." *Journal of Electronic Resources Librarianship* 21, no. 3/4 (2009): 206–12.

Taylor, Donald, Frances Dodd, and James Murphy. "Open-Source Electronic Resource Management System: A Collaborative Implementation." *Serials Librarian* 58, no. 1/4 (Apr. 2010): 61–72.

Trainer, Cindi, and Jason Price. "Rethinking Library Linking: Breathing New Life into OpenULR." *Library Technology Reports* 46, no. 7 (2010).

Whitle, Marilyn, and Susan Sanders. "E-resources Management: How We Positioned Our Organization to Implement an Electronic Resources Management System." *Journal of Electronic Resources Librarianship* 21, no. 3/4 (2009): 183–91.

Wu, Annie, and Anne M. Mitchell. "Mass Management of E-book Catalog Records: Approaches, Challenges, and Solutions." *Library Resources and Technical Services* 54, no. 3 (July 2012): 164–74.

Notes

1. George Stachokas, "Electronic Resources and Mission Creep: Reorganizing the Library for the Twenty-First Century," *Journal of Electronic Resources Librarianship* 21, no. 3 (2009): 206–12.

2. Nicola J. Cecchino, "A Systematic Approach to Developing an Online Medical Library," *Journal of Electronic Resources in Medical Libraries* 7, no. 3 (2010): 218–27.

3. Rebecca L. Mugridge and Jeff Edmunds, "Batchloading MARC Bibliographic Records: Current Practices and Future Challenges in Large Research Libraries," *Library Resources and Technical Services* 56, no. 3 (July 2012): 155–70.

4. Maria Collins and Jill E. Grogg, "Building a Better ERMS," *Library Journal* 136, no. 4 (Mar. 1, 2011): 22–28.

5. Timothy D. Jewel et al., "Electronic Resource Management Report of the DLF ERM Initiative" (Aug. 2004), http://old.diglib.org/pubs/dlf102/ERMFINAL.pdf.

6. Tim Jewell et al., *Making Good on the Promise of ERM: A Standards and Best Practices Discussion Paper* (Baltimore: NISO, 2012), www.niso.org/publications/white_papers/erm_promise.

7. EDItEUR, ONIX, ONIS-PL, www.editeur.org/21/ONIX-PL.

8. Marshall Breeding, *Knowledge Base and Link Resolver Study: General Findings* (May 1, 2012), www.kb.se/dokument/Knowledgebase_linkresolver_study.pdf.

9. NISO/UKSG KBART Working Group, *KBART: Knowledge Bases and Related Tools: A Recommended Practice of the National Information Standards Organization (NISO) and UKSG, NISO-RP-9-2010* (Baltimore: NISO, 2010), www.uksg.org/sites/uksg.org/files/KBART_Phase_I_Recommended_Practice.pdf.

10. Janet A. Crum, "One-Stop Shopping for Journal Holdings," in *Electronic Resource Management in Libraries: Research and Practice*, ed. Holly Yu and Scott Breivold, 213–34 (Hershey, PA: Information Science Reference, 2008), 219.

11. Christine L. Ferguson, Maria D. D. Collins, and Jill E. Grogg, "Finding the Perfect E-journal Access Solution . . . the Hard Way," *Technical Services Quarterly* 23, no. 4 (2006): 27–50.

12. Library of Congress, Cataloging Distribution Service, *CONSER Editing Guide* (Washington, DC: Library of Congress, 1994).

13. Program for Cooperative Cataloging, *CONSER Cataloging Manual*, Module 31 Remote Access Electronic Serials (Online Serials), March 2012 draft, www.loc.gov/aba/pcc/conser/pdf/Module31.pdf.

14. Becky Culbertson, Yael Mandelstam, and George Prager, *Provider-Neutral E-monograph MARC Records Guide* (includes revisions to September 2011) (Washington, DC: Program for Cooperative Cataloging, 2009), www.loc.gov/aba/pcc/bibco/documents/PN-Guide.pdf.

15. Chris Armstrong and Ray Londsdale, "Challenges in Managing E-books Collections in UK Academic Libraries," *Library Collection, Acquisitions, and Technical Services* 29, no. 1 (2005): 33–50.

16. Ibid.; Lucia Snowhill, "E-books and Their Future in Academic Libraries: An Overview," *D-Lib Magazine* 7, no. 7/8 (July/Aug. 2001), www.dlib.org/dlib/july01/snowhill/07snowhill.html.

17. Primary Research Group, *Library Use of eBooks, 2012 Edition* (New York: Primary Research Group, 2011).

18. Primary Research Group, *Library Use of Video and Audio* (New York; Primary Research Group, 2011).

19. Judy Luther, *Streamlining Book Metadata Workflow* (Baltimore: NISO; Dublin, OH: OCLC, 2009), www.niso.org/publications/white_papers/StreamlineBookMetadataWorkflowWhite Paper.pdf.

20. Primary Research Group, *Library Use of eBooks, 2012 Edition.*

21. Roger C. Schonfeld and Ross Housewright, *Documents for a Digital Democracy: A Model for the Federal Depository Library Program in the 21st Century* (New York: Ithaka S+R, 2009), www.arl.org/bm~doc/documents-for-a-digital-democracy.pdf.

22. Luther, *Streamlining Book Metadata Workflow,* 10.

23. Kristin E. Martin and Kavita Mundle, "Cataloging E-books and Vendor Records: A Case Study at the University of Illinois at Chicago," *Library Resources and Technical Services* 54, no. 4 (Oct. 2010): 227–37, quote on 232.

24. MarcEdit: Your Complete Free MARC Editing Utility, http://people.oregonstate.edu/~reeset/marcedit.

25. Andrew Nagy, "Defining the Next-Generation Catalog," *Library Technology Reports* 47, no. 7 (Oct. 2011): 11–15.

26. Marshall Breeding, "Automation Marketplace 2012: Agents of Change," *The Digital Shift* (March 29, 2012), www.thedigitalshift.com/2012/03/ils/automation-marketplace-2012-agents-of-change.

CHAPTER 7

BUDGETING AND FINANCIAL CONSIDERATIONS

LIBRARIANS HAVE VIEWED funding for libraries as insufficient for many years. User expectations for access to e-content and the increasing costs of providing that access have compounded this sense of hardship. McKenrick calls this problem "the digital squeeze."[1] Faced with the priority that users place on e-content and the cost of this content, libraries need to plan and manage their budgets as effectively as possible to maximize their available dollars. This chapter explores budgeting—the process of planning and managing collections budgets—and options for forecasting and managing expenditures.

Librarians use the term *budget* to mean two things: a plan (sometimes called a budget document) for the use of money available in a budget cycle, called the fiscal year; and the amount available and allocated in that year. Libraries approach their fiscal year with a plan designed to meet their user community's needs and institutional priorities through the equitable distribution of money that will cover expenditures during the year. Before the fiscal year begins, libraries develop a budget that reflects expected revenues, allocations, and projected expenditures. Available funds are allocated to cover types of expenditures. A library budget usually consists of an operating budget, which covers ongoing expenses necessary to operate the library, and a materials budget, which may be called the acquisitions budget, collections budget, information and access budget, or something else. The personnel budget may be part of the operating budget or managed as a separate personnel budget.

Most nonprofit organizations are required to use fund accounting to track allocations and expenditures. In this practice, funds are classified for accounting and reporting purposes in accordance with the regulations, restrictions, or limitations imposed by the governing board or sources outside the library, or in accordance with activities or objectives specified by donors.

MATERIALS BUDGETS

Preparing a materials budget begins with allocating available money to fund lines. In addition, an annual budget may include fund balances and encumbrances brought forward from the previous year, if permitted by the parent organization. A fund balance is the dollars allocated but unexpended at the end of a fiscal year. Encumbrances represent the projected cost of orders that have been placed but for which the items have not yet been received or access activated and for which no invoice has been paid. An encumbrance is recorded as soon as the order is placed and serves to record the obligation for future payment. When the item is received or access activated and the invoice processed for payment, the encumbrance is cleared and the actual cost of the material is recorded as an expenditure. If encumbrances are present at the end of the fiscal year, unexpended funds must be held in escrow and carried forward until payments for outstanding orders are made. The budget cycle ends with reconciliation of allocations, expenditure, and encumbrances. In many libraries, unexpended balances are carried forward into the next fiscal year, where they may remain in fund lines or be scooped into a central fund.

Some libraries' parent organizations do not permit carrying forward unspent balances and recover these centrally. In addition, some parent organizations do not permit carrying forward encumbrances, meaning that outstanding orders must be cancelled and placed again in the next fiscal year. These two practices place additional pressure on a library to monitor and manage budgets effectively during the budget cycle.

Another practice that varies in libraries is the extent to which funds can be moved from one budget line to another within a budget period. Some parent organizations may prohibit, for example, moving salary savings from unfilled positions to the materials budget, but they may permit moving money from one fund line to another within the materials budget. Understanding the degree of flexibility in transferring funds during the year is important when funds are allocated to different lines at the beginning of the cycle.

Responsibility for materials budgets requires constant monitoring to ensure that allocations are spent down by the end of the year and no deficits are created. Funds must be allocated effectively before the year begins to ensure that sufficient dollars are available to pay annual subscription invoices. Allocations should be spent prudently during the course of the budget cycle.

Large unspent balances can create an assumption that these funds are not needed. A well-crafted budget and judicious expenditures become an internal control that can measure operating effectiveness and performance.

LINE-ITEM AND FUND ACCOUNTING

Within the materials budget, most libraries allocate funds to different types of expenditures using a line-item format. This varies from library to library, depending on the library's definition of types or categories of expense. Typically, libraries have allocated materials budgets to nondiscretionary fund lines and discretionary fund lines. Nondiscretionary fund lines are set up for purchases that happen automatically—that is, known fixed expenses. Examples are serial subscriptions and blanket orders. Nondiscretionary purchases imply a continuing annual commitment against the materials budget. Discretionary purchases are items that are selected individually and do not fall within an existing blanket order plan, serial subscription, or other nondiscretionary purchase.

Libraries may consider approval plans as nondiscretionary or create separate fund lines solely for approval plans. With approval plans, print books are shipped automatically or e-book access is turned on automatically according to the library's profile. Annual expenditures vary on the number and cost of books provided through approval plans, but many libraries use previous years' expenditures to allocate funds for the next year's projected approval plan expenditures. Some libraries may consider approval plan expenditures as discretionary because the library can reduce the size of the plan or turn it off at any point. Dividing allocations between nondiscretionary, discretionary, and perhaps approval fund lines before the fiscal year starts ensures that sufficient funds are available to cover expected bills as they arrive during the year.

Libraries have used granular fund accounting to facilitate equitable distribution of funds, to hold individual librarians responsible for fund lines and accountable for prudent financial management, and to report to various parties how funds are expended. For example, a public library might have two fund lines for children's materials—discretionary and nondiscretionary. If the library has a large budget, the discretionary allocation might be further subdivided into picture books, early readers, chapter books, and young adult literature, or into fiction and nonfiction. An academic library might have fund lines for arts, humanities, social science, and science. A larger academic library might further divide the arts into performing arts, visual arts, art history, and so on.

Some libraries use their materials budget for expenses associated with the acquisition and management of or access to resources. These might be binding and other preservation and conservation treatments, vendor service charges, postage and handling fees, catalog records, shelf-ready processing, institution memberships, consortial fees, e-content hosting fees, or electronic services and management tools. Some libraries use materials budgets to pay ILL and document delivery charges. Money may be allocated to separate fund lines for each of these expenses (e.g., to a "utilities fund" to cover the cost of electronic services and management tools such as the library's ERM system) or may be included in an existing fund line. For example, catalog records may be purchased with the same fund line that covers the cost of e-book packages.

Allocations within the larger categories of nondiscretionary and discretionary may be further distributed to subject areas, user groups or reading levels (children, adults, etc.), locations (individual schools within a district, branches, campuses), or format (print, microform, audio and visual media, e-resources). Greater granularity in allocating funds (i.e., defining subjects or user groups narrowly and creating more fund lines to manage allocation to them) supports more detailed expenditure tracking but can make fund management more complex.

Regardless of the approach to allocation that a library takes, the goal is always to allocate funds to meet the needs of library users, ensure that funds are available to meet expenditures during the fiscal year, and support the mission and goals of the library. Equitable distribution of funds, whether according to subjects, user groups, formats, or library locations, continues to test the skills of collections librarians.

ALLOCATING FOR E-RESOURCES

More than ten years ago, researchers reported that practices for allocating materials budgets were archaic, geared to print resource acquisition, and in need of radical updating.[2] In the intervening years, no best practice has emerged. Libraries continue to struggle with the most effective way to prepare and manage budgets that cover access to and purchase of e-content. Doing so successfully presents several challenges. Ensuring that sufficient funds are allocated appropriately to cover known and projected expenditures can be difficult, especially when existing budgetary practices are geared to print resource acquisition. The first decisions in preparing a budget are which type of fund lines to use and whether new fund lines should be created. The familiar distinction between monographs as discretionary purchases and serials as nondiscretionary purchases may not apply. Libraries that traditionally have tracked expenditures at a granular level may find this more difficult when many titles supporting different subjects and serving various user groups appear on a single invoice or are part of a package. Determining allocation amounts and appropriate fund lines for patron-driven acquisitions and pay-per-view can be difficult, especially if the library has no retrospective data on which to base future allocations.

Are e-resources nondiscretionary or discretionary expenditures? E-journals and databases continue to fall logically within the category of nondiscretionary purchases, as did their print counterparts. The library receives an annual bill for the subscription, which, like that for print journals and indexes, generally increases each year. Platform or hosting fees for this content typically are part of the amount billed. Individually selected e-books often are considered discretionary purchases. A complication arises when the library is subscribing to a package of e-books for which funds must be set aside at the beginning of each fiscal year. Subscriptions to e-book packages may have a recurring annual base fee with supplementary charges for each e-book added to the package during the year. Even when the library is purchasing the e-books from a publisher or vendor and not paying an annual subscription fee, it may need to budget for recurring annual hosting fees.

Budget models vary in how they handle allocation of and responsibility for expending funds on e-resources. Some libraries have a single central fund line used for all e-resources, opting to track purchases by format only. This model can be found in libraries that have a single selector and those that have several. A single separate fund can stress the priority of e-resources to the organization and make tracking expenditures easier, but it also can focus on their separateness from other selection and management activities. An advantage of this approach is simplicity, but details about how and on what funds are expended are lost. Libraries that take this expedient approach often need to track expense detail in another manner. At the other end of the continuum is the model in which all funds are allocated to separate budget lines, with individual librarians managing these lines as they do for other library materials. This might be called a format-agnostic approach and provides detailed tracking of expenses by subject or user group served in a manner that supports easy reporting to interested parties. Librarians with narrow selection responsibilities may make cooperative purchases with other selectors by pooling funds, but in this model no resources are funded centrally. If, however, e-journals are part of a package from an aggregator or a single publisher, separating and tracking costs of individual titles can be difficult for collections librarians and library acquisitions and accounting staff. Many libraries combine budgeting approaches, retaining some money in a central fund for resources of system-wide interest (perhaps a general periodical index and associated full-text file, encyclopedias, or aggregator packages) and allocating funds to individual budget lines for more narrowly focused titles.

Tracking allocations and expenditures at a more granular level becomes more difficult and more labor-intensive when many titles supporting different subjects and serving various user groups appear on a single invoice, are part of a package, or are covered in the same database. Many e-resources are no longer selected and managed by individuals on a title-by-title basis. Tracking titles that are added through macro-selection (i.e., en bloc) no longer serves an accountability function because an individual librarian is no longer making decisions about the fund lines for which he or she is responsible. Teasing titles apart and assigning them to separate fund lines for tracking, even if possible, adds significant work to acquisitions and accounting activities. In response, some libraries have simplified their fund structures.[3] They may reduce the granularity and thus the number of fund lines, or create new funds for packages and databases that cover multiple subjects. For example, a library might create a general e-serials fund or a general e-content budget, unattributed by subject. A 2011 survey of 448 U.S. academic libraries of all sizes found that 63 percent budgeted for e-books by including them in a general digital content budget.[4] Forty-three percent included e-books in the print resources budgets, and another 17 percent had a separate line for e-books only. The smallest libraries used a general acquisitions budget that covered all formats. No best practice exists for allocating budgets for e-content. Each library must compare the benefits gained from using narrowly defined fund lines and the cost in staff time to maintain them.

Managing the financial aspects of demand-driven acquisitions such as pay-per-view and patron-driven acquisition can be complicated, especially if a library has no retrospective data on which to base future allocations. Deciding the amount to allocate, the appropriate fund lines to use, and mechanisms for monitoring and controlling expenditures can be difficult. Experience has shown that users often treat unmediated pay-per-view and patron-driven acquisition as a never-ending buffet.[5] Many libraries have found that use quickly outstrips the funds that have been allocated.

Pay-per-view requires payment in exchange for permission to read an individual document, usually an individual article, book, or book chapter.

Libraries often take this approach as a less costly alternative to subscriptions when it is projected to be less expensive than the cost of an annual subscription and a faster and potentially cheaper alternative than ILL. Libraries that use materials budget funds to support ILL and document delivery might support pay-per-view within the allocation for these services. The logic behind this budgeting approach is that the library is providing just-in-time access to meet users' immediate needs instead of purchasing content "just in case" a user may want that content at some future date. A library may set up a separate fund line to support pay-per-view, using money redirected from the allocations that previously supported subscriptions or book purchases. Some publishers that offer pay-per-view give libraries the option of setting up deposit accounts against which it is charged. Some libraries expect the patron to bear the cost. Regardless of who pays for pay-per-view, an important consideration for libraries is the annual administration fee the supplier charges.

Patron-driven acquisition began as an option for acquiring print books and has expanded to include e-books. This approach depends on a library loading records in its local catalog for titles from a particular publisher or book vendor. The library does not purchase the item until patrons have viewed it a specified number of times. A variation that combines pay-per-view and patron-driven acquisition is often referred to as the short-term loan or rental option. In this model, the library rents the item (usually a book) at a discounted price, perhaps 10 percent of the list price. When a set number of rentals is reached, the library purchases the book. Not all publishers or vendors offer short-term loans, and those that do may not permit using the cumulated rental fees toward the purchase of the title. Although a poorly managed patron-driven acquisition program runs the risk of depleting allocated funds quickly, an effective program can develop a collection that meets user needs and saves money. Way and Garrison determined that the average cost per use of all e-books acquired through patron-driven acquisition at Grand Valley State University (Michigan) Libraries was $6.57, compared to an average cost per use of $46.40 for librarian-purchased e-books and an average cost of $20.00 per ILL book.[6]

Libraries allocate for pay-per-view and patron-driven acquisition at the beginning of the budget cycle, unless they are undertaking a pilot project. Allocations for patron-driven acquisition are usually redirected from discretionary budget lines. Allocations for pay-per-view may be redirected from serials (i.e., nondiscretionary) budget lines. Determining the appropriate amount to allocate has been a significant problem for libraries. Many libraries have been caught short because of the extremely fast pace of spending that uncontrolled patron-driven models often generate. If controls are not in place, libraries can find that the allocation is spent before the fiscal year ends. If that happens, a library must either allocate additional funds or cut off the service, disadvantaging users during the rest of the year. Libraries have used pilot projects to get a sense of the usage volume these models can generate.

Pay-per-view and patron-driven acquisition can be managed in various ways. Many libraries control use of pay-per-view by defining the user categories that have access or requiring that requests over a set price cap be mediated by library staff. Libraries can set parameters governing the patron-driven acquisition records that are loaded into the catalog, limiting by publisher, reading level, date of publication, or price. Some academic libraries limit patron acquisitions to faculty, staff, and graduate students. As with pay-per-view, a library can require librarian mediation before a patron-driven title is ordered or require librarian review of titles above a price cap. Some libraries load records only for titles that would have been provided on an approval plan. Some vendors offer to provide a monthly title list for librarian review before records are loaded in the catalog. Both these approaches limit patron-driven acquisition to titles the library likely would have added but position the titles to be vetted by the user community before being ordered—another version of just-in-time service instead of acquiring materials just in case a patron might want them in the future.

An essential concept in budgeting for patron-driven acquisition is that it should be understood as part of routine collection building and not viewed as a supplement or special initiative. It is an alternative to librarian selection of content and should be funded as part of the library's overall collection plan. Funds can come from various fund lines or be allocated first before the remaining money is distributed to fund lines. If the library has run pilot projects on these two models, the amount that should be allocated can be extrapolated from activity during the project.

TRACKING EXPENDITURES

Demonstrating accountability to parent organizations and funding agencies is an important responsibility. Libraries often seek to prove effective stewardship of the funds they receive by reporting what was acquired with these funds. Counting physical materials acquired, current serial subscriptions, and funds expended by subjects, genre, and user community served are long-established measures of library performance. Although libraries and their parent organizations are increasingly looking beyond quantitative measures to demonstrate outcomes and the degree to which the organization's goals are achieved, user groups often want to know dollars spent and titles acquired in their area of interest, whether it is large-print books, DVDs, or materials that support the English department. Reducing the number of fund lines can hamper this type of reporting. For example, access to several hundred e-journals might be provided through an aggregator's database and the single invoice paid with a general e-serials fund. Unless the library has implemented ways to map the individual journal titles to fund lines or subject areas, detailed reporting is no longer possible. Libraries in this situation should discuss new ways of tracking acquisitions and expenditures with the groups that have previously received these data.

Other metrics often requested are total expenditures for e-content and the percentage of all materials expenditures devoted to e-content. Such expenditure information is more readily available to a library that allocates by format. If a library has taken the format-agnostic approach, one option for retrieving these data is to use subaccounts or subfunds in the library's accounting system or ILS to indicate e-content. Another option is to code orders by order type (firm order, approval plan, subscription, etc.) and format type (print book, e-book, e-journal, map, sheet music, etc.). This latter approach requires carefully defined terms, clear understanding of how to use them, and well-trained staff to do so. When either option is implemented, most accounting systems and ILSs can generate various reports showing expenditures for e-content.

Part of the challenge in reporting statistics is the rapidly evolving nature of e-content. The Association for Research Libraries (ARL) has explored effective and meaningful ways to measure expenditures for e-resources since 1996.[7] Although ARL members are the 126 largest research libraries in North America, their statistics-gathering practice illustrates the complexity of collecting meaningful data about e-resources. The 2010–11 ARL statistics questionnaire requested familiar data points, such as volumes held, volumes added, titles held, and titles added. The latter two categories included e-books and e-journals along with other formats. "Monographic volumes purchased" included e-books that were "electronic manifestations of physical entities and/or units."[8] In addition, the ARL worksheet for supplementary statistics requested information about the number of e-books held and expenditures for e-books, which are subsets of data reported in the general questionnaire.[9] The questionnaire also requested detailed data on electronic expenditures (a subset of total materials expenditures), to be reported for one-time electronic resource purchases and ongoing electronic resource purchases. Even these two categories are not as clear-cut as one might assume. One-time electronic resources are defined as "not serials," with periodical backfiles, literature collections, and one-time costs for JSTOR membership given as examples. Ongoing electronic resources are defined as subscription-based serials. Examples are paid subscriptions for electronic journals and indexes/abstracts available via the Internet, CD-ROM serials, and annual access fees for resources purchased on a one-time basis, such as literature collections and JSTOR membership. A simple way to think about these categories is to view them as discretionary and nondiscretionary expenditures for e-content. Regardless of how and to whom a library reports e-content statistics, consistency in definitions is important for comparative and trending purposes.

FORECASTING AND MANAGING EXPENDITURES

Good budget planning depends on accurate estimates (to the extent possible) of what materials will cost in the future. Gathering information about how costs may change is key to deciding the amounts to allocate, yet doing so for e-resources often feels like discerning the future with a crystal ball—both murky and suspect.[10] No standard predictive tools for e-book and e-subscription prices exist. Even if such tools were available, the amounts libraries actually pay usually depend less on the list price and more on the negotiations in which libraries and their suppliers engage and the way that publishers, aggregators, and suppliers interact to set prices.

Projecting next year's prices often begins by reviewing historical prices for trends. Historical prices are found in price indexes, which are "a normalized average of prices of a defined set of goods, commodities, or services in a defined region, during a set interval of time," and price surveys.[11] The goal of price indexes is to measure as accurately as possible on a periodic basis the extent of price changes on a similar set of items (serials or books) to document market trends. Two sources measure and track serials prices. The U.S. Periodical Price Index is jointly prepared by the Library Materials Price Index Editorial Board of the Association for Library Collections and Technical Services and Swets Information Services and is published in the *Library and Book Trade Almanac* (formerly *The Bowker Annual*). *Library Journal* also prepares an annual Periodicals Price Survey.[12] Price indexes and surveys usually include tables giving cost histories by Library of Congress subject headings and by disciplines and broad subject areas. The *Library Journal* Periodicals Price Survey includes tables showing periodical prices for high school and small public libraries and for university and college libraries. The American Association of Law Libraries prepares its own price index for legal publications (books, serial publication, legal periodical, etc.), which is available to its members.

These sources have two drawbacks: those dealing with serials have primarily indexed print serial publications (although this is changing) because most of the current work on serials pricing is based on the 1999 NISO *Criteria for Price Indexes for Print Library Materials.*[13] In addition, the data reported may be one to two years old. Librarians should note that subscription prices are publishers' list prices, excluding publisher discount or vendor services charges.

A complicating factor in tracking and projecting e-journal prices is the range of pricing models. Models include online-only, print-plus-free-online, print-plus-online for an additional charge, tiered pricing (which varies by the type of library, size of user community and usage in the previous year, and concentration in specific disciplines), and Big Deal packages. In the latter, increases in the cost of the package each year are determined by the contract in place with the library.

The *Library and Book Trade Almanac* began including price indexes for e-books in the 2012 edition. These show data on current average prices and recent price increases but do not predict future trends. E-book prices remain volatile for several reasons. For example, when one vendor ingested a large backlist of e-books in a single year, the number of titles spiked that year. Because these were discounted because of their age, the index for e-books showed a price decline. Another variable is the business model and purchase option in effect. Libraries may acquire access to e-books from a publisher or aggregator; participate in a consortial deal or work independently; purchase in perpetuity, subscribe for a year, rent access case by case, or participate in a supplier's short-term loan option; buy a package of titles or buy title by title; or license for one concurrent user or license for any number of concurrent users. Libraries may pay a platform fee. For example, many e-book models increase the retail price by as much as 50 to 100 percent for a multiuser license. The variety of options affects predicting future prices in ways not found when projecting print books prices.

BookStats, published annually by the Association of American Publishers Book Industry Study Group, and *Publisher's Weekly* provide statistical information about pricing and publishing trends. The intended audience for both is the U.S. publishing and retail industry, but certain data points are of interest to libraries. For example, the 2012 *BookStats* reported that e-books ranked as the top individual format for adult fiction in 2011.[14]

Additional resources are annual prices projections that subscription agents and book vendors produce, usually in the fall, to aid their customers in preparing budgets for the next year. Most of these projections are announced in the library literature and are freely available. A library can do fairly well projecting next year's e-journal expenses by consulting these sources. If, for example, a subscription agent predicts a 5.9 percent increase for all serials titles and the *Library Journal* Periodicals Price Survey predicts a 6.1 percent, then a library should expect its overall serials costs to increase by at least 6.0 percent. However, as the compilers of "Prices of U.S. and Foreign Published Materials" in the *Library and Book Trade Almanac* observed, the indexes, "are useful benchmarks against which local costs can be compared, but because they reflect retail prices in the aggregate, they are not a substitute for cost data that reflect the collecting patterns of individual libraries and they are not a substitute for specific cost studies."[15]

Many subscription agents and book vendors provide customized budget analysis reports, which estimate annual expenditures and specific price projections for a customer on the basis of previous activity. Agents create a report using the list of journal titles the library orders through the vendor. Book vendors provide total volume of activity for print books and e-books a customer acquires through the vendor. Further breakdowns by number of e-books delivered through patron-driven acquisition, short-term loans, and e-books provided on an approval plan may be available. Some book vendors report average cost of an e-book by publisher.

With data from price surveys and indexes, annual price projections from agents and vendors, and customized agent and vendor reports, a library can make an informed prediction about expenditures in the next budget cycle. Few libraries, however, are able to maintain the number and types of materials they acquire and to which they subscribe from one year to the next because their budgets do not increase at the same rate as materials prices.

Controlling Costs

Price indexes and surveys show that the cost of library materials continues to increase. Price predictions make clear that this trend is not abating. To cope, libraries need either increased allocations or decreased expenses to meet the limitations imposed by the budgets they receive. Few libraries are seeing budget increases. A study of public library funding conducted in 2011–12 found that 56.7 percent of public libraries reported flat or decreased budgets.[16] School library media centers expected continuing budget cuts in 2012–13, with elementary schools expecting a 2.9 percent reduction, middle schools expecting a 4.6 percent reduction, and high schools expecting a 2.4 percent reduction.[17] McKenrick's study of 730 libraries of all types (excluding schools) found that 77 percent of the libraries reported budget reductions in 2011.[18] Even those libraries fortunate enough to receive budget increases of 3 percent (the amount the U.S Consumer Price Index increased in 2011) cannot keep up with materials cost increases of 5–6 percent. Librarians have to balance the shortfalls this situation produces while striving to meet growing user expectations for e-content.

Several options are available, but none is a perfect solution. Libraries may reduce allocations for books to protect allocations for subscriptions. This is a temporary fix because over time the allocations for books will be consumed and the cost of subscriptions will still continue to increase. Eventually, most libraries face cancellation projects. A first step might be to eliminate print and print-plus-online subscriptions in favor of e-only subscriptions. A second might be to reduce the number of simultaneous users. If more than one user accessing the resource at the same time is unlikely, a library might change to a single user model. Some libraries have determined that a free database, even with a less user-friendly interface, is acceptable and the commercial product can be cancelled. Many libraries find they are duplicating content in aggregator databases and decide to retain only those with the heaviest use or the most unique full text. When access to e-content must be cancelled, libraries should make decisions informed by usage data and evaluate cost per use.

Libraries are considering alternatives to paid subscriptions. They may look at access-oriented models in which subscriptions are cancelled and the library relies increasingly on ILL and pay-per-view. Some libraries are looking toward open access as a viable alternative to paid subscriptions. Research that studied peer-reviewed scientific journal articles published in 2008 found that overall 20.4 percent were available via open access.[19] Subsequent research determined that 23 percent of scholarly articles in all disciplines published in 2010 were available via open access.[20] Open access is not yet a viable option for all scholarly articles.

Many libraries are reconsidering their participation in Big Deals. The early Big Deal offers tendered by publishers were based on a library's historic expenditures for the publisher's print journals. Big Deals generally require a multiyear (usually three) agreement and limit cancellations. Big Deal agreements can quickly consume a large portion of the acquisition budget and consequently narrow options when budget constraints force cancellations. Botero, Carrico, and Tennant reported that some packages individually consume 10 or 20 percent of the overall collection budget, with the total impact of all publisher packages sometimes surpassing 50 percent of the library's materials budget.[21] Big Deals often consist of a publisher's entire title list. By providing such an extensive list of titles at a discounted price, this kind of package can increase usage and lower per-article cost.[22] The Big Deal has supporters and detractors, but most agree on the need for greater flexibility to control content inclusion, swap and replace titles, cancel titles, and access titles following cancellation.

Because of the multiyear nature of most Big Deal contracts, libraries usually have to wait until the contract is up for renewal before making changes. Some libraries have had success renegotiating these contracts before the term of the contract ends if they or their parent organization has declared a financial exigency or simply faces severe budget problems. Libraries may be able to lower prices or lower the annual price increase cap. Many libraries have decided not to renew one or more Big Deals and renewed only the most heavily used e-journals in the package, relying on ILL and pay-per-view to supply their users with content from the cancelled titles.

Narrowing the criteria for e-books (and their records loaded into the catalog) available for patron-driven acquisition can reduce expenditures by limiting the universe from which patrons can select titles. Limiting the categories of patrons who can initiate such purchases can control the volume of titles ordered. These approaches, however, can negate the goal of most such programs—to engage patrons in selecting the materials they find of greatest value and to build a collection just in time instead of just in case. Mouw at the University of Chicago reported that half of that university's monograph budget in 2010 was devoted to patron-driven acquisition and speculated that it might reach 100 percent.[23]

Other options offer ways that libraries can stretch their budgets. Some vendors offer deposit accounts, which can streamline payment routines and reduce paperwork. Some pay interest credits on deposit accounts if the average balance in a month exceeds a specified cap. Reducing the number of book vendors and consolidating orders with one or two vendors may reduce service charges and increase the discounts. Consolidating orders with fewer subscription agents also can reduce service charges. Some serials agents accept prepayments toward the annual renewal invoice. If the library and its parent agency permit prepayments, libraries may be able to use money available at the end of the fiscal year to reduce or prevent carrying forward funds. Some vendors and agents offer discounts for prepayments.

Consortia

One common means of stretching a library's materials budget is to purchase e-content through a consortium. Research conducted in December 2011 found that 89 percent of 730 responding libraries of all types (excluding schools) belonged to at least one consortium or library network and 53 percent belonged to three or more.[24] All but one of seventy-three respondents to a 2010 ARL survey reported that they belonged to consortia "for the primary purpose of acquiring commercially available e-resources."[25] The Primary Research Group reported in 2012 that 43.92 percent of library spending on scholarly journals occurred through deals negotiated by consortia.[26] Consortia accounted for even higher percentages of e-book purchases: 64.4 percent of e-book purchases by public libraries and 46.5 percent of purchases by academic libraries.[27] *Library Journal* found variant data, reporting that 59 percent of 339 academic libraries surveyed in 2012 were part of a consortium license program for e-books and another 5 percent planned to join one in the future.[28] Most libraries use consortia to leverage their e-content budgets.

Consortia gather multiple buyers that can combine purchases into one transaction for the publisher or distributer. E-content suppliers have found they can sell more because libraries often purchase content through a consortium that they would not purchase directly. Some consortia offer multiple services, such as a union catalog, staff training, research sharing, and digital repositories. Some consortia function solely as buying pools. By combining purchases, consortium members can have access to publishers' discounts not made available to individual institutions. One example of consortial buying is the Wisconsin Public Library Consortium, which is collaboratively purchasing e-books, audiobooks, videos, and music. Residents across Wisconsin, regardless of location, can download the content. The group purchase allows smaller libraries access to more materials than they could afford on their own. In 2012 all seventeen Wisconsin library systems and their 387 member public libraries contributed $700,000, which was combined with another $300,000 from Library Services and Technology Act funds to create an e-book buying pool.[29] As another example, TexShare, a consortium of Texas libraries of all types and sizes administered by the Texas State Library and Archives Commission, shares print and electronic materials, purchases online resources, and combines staff expertise. TexShare reported that the 685 libraries participating in the TexShare database program in 2011–12 would have spent $101,982,797 to acquire access to the forty-nine database subscriptions that were purchased by the Texas State Library and Archives Commission for $5,977,061.[30]

Consortia can do more than just leverage a library's available funds for acquiring access to and managing e-content. If member dues support consortium staffing, another benefit may be centralized license negotiation on behalf of the consortium members, saving effort in the individual libraries. Some standard license terms may be relaxed for consortium members. For example, licenses for e-book packages may be amended to permit members to share e-books, loosening the document delivery and ILL limitations in most agreements. Some consortia centralize various aspects of technical work and may work together to acquire, edit, and load bibliographic records for consortial purchases.

Working through a consortium to acquire and subscribe to e-content has drawbacks as well. All consortium members may not be interested in a product. Fewer participants usually means a smaller discount for those members that do join in the deal. Reaching closure can be time-consuming because of differing member perspectives, needs, and interests. Some libraries or their parent organizations may require local contract review before signing the agreement, negating potential savings gained by centralized licensing. Libraries may not be able to agree on the business model. Issues such as the number of copies of an e-book and options for simultaneous use may be stumbling blocks. Definitions of an acceptable bibliographic record may vary. Libraries that participate in several consortia that acquire different packages may find unnecessary and undesirable duplications of titles. Stern suggests that complexity of acquiring and managing e-books is multiplied at the consortium level.[31]

PROS AND CONS OF ACQUIRING
E-CONTENT THROUGH CONSORTIA

Pros

- Group discounts can reduce the initial cost of e-content.
- Consortia provide access to e-content that libraries cannot afford otherwise.
- Consortial pressure may be able to control inflationary increases.

- Members can have increased opportunity to choose from existing and new resources.
- Libraries can increase buying power by leveraging available funds to acquire access to more content.
- Centralized licensing can reduce institutional involvement in negotiations.
- More attractive licensing terms may be negotiated for the consortium members.
- A collaborative approach can improve the quality of vendor-supplied bibliographic records.

Cons

- Not all consortium members may decide to purchase a product, reducing the discount the supplier is willing to provide.
- Not all libraries or their parent organizations may be willing to turn over contract negotiation to the consortium staff.
- Not all suppliers have pricing models for consortia.
- Reaching agreement about which libraries will purchase a product and the amount each will pay can be a slow process because of the number of libraries that must be coordinated.
- Packages may include titles of little or no interest to the library.
- Some suppliers reject billing through consortia and require direct invoicing to libraries.
- Controlling costs requires a combination of approaches. Each library must look carefully at its own budget and the needs of its users to develop be best mix of tactics.

SUMMARY

Budgeting for e-resources requires balancing user community needs and institutional priorities within the context of available funds. Libraries seek to allocate a budget so that money is available to cover expenses during the budget cycle. Most libraries use line-item budgets and fund accounting as a means of internal control.

Allocating for e-resource acquisition and access begins with deciding the appropriate type and number of fund lines. An important question that must be resolved is how granular a system of fund lines is desirable or needed and whether the effort to maintain it is justified by the data that can be retrieved. Identifying continuing commitments and allocating to the appropriate fund lines are critical to ensure that sufficient funds are available when invoices are received.

Patron-driven acquisition and pay-per-view present challenges because many libraries do not have sufficient history to project expenditures for these services. Libraries usually are expected to track and report expenditures by type and category as a measure of accountability. The manner in which this is done depends on the financial management systems the library uses and the needs of those to whom reports are submitted.

Forecasting prices and acquisition activity is critical to creating a viable budget. Price indexes and surveys, vendor and agent reports, and local historical data are useful tools. Trend data reveal that materials costs increase faster than most libraries' budgets can accommodate. Libraries look to cancelling subscriptions, renegotiating Big Deals, relying on delivery models in lieu of subscriptions, and joining consortia to help control and reduce expenditures. No perfect solution exists, and each library must approach budget development and fiscal management in the manner that best matches its own user community, mission, and financial situation.

Suggested Readings

Ashmore, Beth, and Jill E. Grogg. "The Art of the Deal: The Power and Pitfalls of Consortial Negotiation." *Searcher* 17, no. 3 (Mar. 2009): 40–47.

Bergstrom, Theodore C. "Librarians and the Terrible Fix: Economics of the Big Deal." *Serials* 23, no. 2 (July 2012): 77–82.

Best, Rickey D. "Is the 'Big Deal' Dead?" *Serials Librarian* 57, no. 4 (Nov./Dec. 2009): 353–63.

Burnette, Elizabeth S. "Budgeting and Acquisition." In *Managing the Transition from Print to Electronic Journals and Resources: A Guide for Library and Information Professionals*, ed. Maria D. D. Collins and Patrick L. Carr, 3–27. New York: Routledge, 2008.

Busby, Lorraine. "Our Friends Are Killing Us." *Serials Librarian* 61, no. 2 (2011): 160–67.

Cleary, Colleen. "Why the 'Big Deal' Continues to Persist." *Serials Librarian* 57, no. 4 (2009): 364–79.

Cryer, Emma, and Karen S. Grigg. "Consortia and Journal Package Renewal: Evolving Trends in the 'Big Package Deal'?" *Journal of Electronic Resources in Medical Libraries* 8, no. 1 (2011): 22–34.

Dinkins, Debbi. "Allocating Academic Library Budgets: Adapting Historical Data Models at One University Library." *Collection Management* 36, no. 2 (2011): 119–30.

Hodges, Dracine, Cyndi Preston, and Marsha J. Hamilton. "Patron-Initiated Collection Development: Progress of a Paradigm Shift." *Collection Management* 35, no. 3/4 (2010): 208–21.

Howard, Jennifer. "Libraries Abandon Expensive 'Big Deal' Subscription Packages to Multiple Journals." *Chronicle of Higher Education* (July 11, 2011). http://chronicle.com/article/Libraries-Abandon-Expensive/128220.

Kusik, James P., and Mark A. Vargas. "Improving Electronic Resources through Holistic Budgeting." *Journal of Electronic Resources Librarianship* 21, no. 3/4 (2009): 200–205.

Lippincott, Sarah Kalikman, et al. "Librarian, Publisher, and Vendor Perspectives on Consortial E-book Purchasing: The Experience of the TRLN Beyond Print Summit," *Serials Review* 38, no. 1 (Mar. 2012): 3–11.

McKee, Anne E. "Consortial Licensing Issues." *Journal of Library Administration* 42, no. 3/4 (2005): 129–41.

Nabe, Jonathan, and David C. Fowler. "Leaving the 'Big Deal': Consequences and Next Steps." *Serials Librarian* 62, no. 1/4 (2012): 59–72.

Pomerantz, Sarah, and Andrew While. "Re-modeling ILS Acquisitions Data to Financially Transition from Print to Digital Formats." *Library Collections, Acquisitions, and Technical Services* 33, no. 1 (2009): 42–49.

Price, Apryl C. "How to Make a Dollar Out of Fifteen Cents: Tips for Electronic Collection Development." *Collection Building* 28, no. 1 (2009): 31–34.

Schell, Lindsey E., Katy Ginanni, and Benjamin Heet, presenters. "Playing the Field: Pay-per-View E-journals and E-books." *Serials Librarian* 58, no. 1/4 (2010): 87–96.

Smith, Debbi A. "Percentage Based Allocation of an Academic Library Materials Budget." *Collection Building* 27, no. 1 (2008): 30–34.

Ward, Suzanne M. *Guide to Implementing and Managing Patron-Driven Acquisitions.* ALCTS Acquisitions Guides Series 16. Chicago: Association for Library Collections and Technical Services and American Library Association, 2012.

Notes

1. Joseph McKenrick, *The Digital Squeeze: Libraries at the Crossroads: The Library Resource Guide Benchmark Study on 2012 Library Spending Plans* (Providence RI: Unisphere Research, 2012), www.libraryresource.com/Downloads/Download.ashx?IssueID=3213.

2. S. Halliday, "Electronic Resources and Academic Library Budgets: The PURCEL Dimension," *Information Services and Use* 21, no. 3/4 (2001): 151–56.

3. Wyoma vanDuinkerken et al., "Creating a Flexible Fund Structure to Meet the Needs and Goals of the Library and Its Users," *Library Collections, Acquisitions, and Technical Services* 32, no. 3/4 (2008): 142–29.

4. *Ebooks: The New Normal: Ebook Penetration and Use in U.S. Academic Libraries, Second Annual Survey* (New York: Library Journal, 2011).

5. Erin S. Fisher and Lisa Kurt, presenters, Sarah Garner, recorder, "Exploring Patron-Driven Access Models for E-journals and E-books," *Serials Librarian* 62, no. 1/4 (2012): 164–169; Tian Ciao Zhang, "Pay-per-View: A Promising Model of E-articles Subscription for Middle/Small Sized Academic Libraries in the Digital Age," *Libraries in the Digital Age (LIDA) Proceedings* 12 (2012), http://ozk.unizd.hr/proceedings/index.php/lida2012/article/view/8/18.

6. Doug Way and Julie Garrison, "Financial Implications of Demand-Driven Acquisitions: A Case Study of the Value of Short-Term Loans," in *Patron-Driven Acquisitions: History and Best Practices*, ed. David A. Swords, 137–56 (Berlin: Walter de Gruyter, 2011).

7. Julia D. Blixrud and Timothy D. Jewell, "Understanding Electronic Resources and Library Materials Expenditures: An Incomplete Picture," *ARL: A Bimonthly Report*, no. 197 (Apr. 1998), www.arl.org/bm~doc/expend.pdf.

8. Association of Research Libraries, "ARL Statistics Questionnaire, 2010–11," www.arl.org/bm~doc/11instruct.pdf, 3.

9. Association for Research Libraries, "ARL Supplementary Statistics 2010–11 Worksheet," www.arl.org/bm~doc/11ssurvey.pdf.

10. Stephen Bosch, Kittie S. Henderson, and Heather Klusendorf, "Polishing the Crystal Ball: Using Historical data to Project Serials Trends and Pricing," *Serials Librarian* 62, no. 1/4 (2012): 87–94.

11. Ibid., 87.

12. See Stephen Bosch and Kittie Henderson, "Coping with the Terrible Twins: Periodical Price Survey 2012," *Library Journal* (Apr. 30, 2012), http://lj.libraryjournal.com/2012/04/funding/coping-with-the-terrible-twins-periodicals-price-survey-2012 for a recent example.

13. National Information Standards Organization, *Criteria for Price Indexes for Print Library Materials*, ANSI/NISO Z39.20 (Baltimore: NISO, 1999).

14. *BookStats: An Annual Comprehensive Study of the U.S. Publishing Industry* [United States] (Association of American Publishers, Book Industry Study Group, 2012).

15. Association for Library Collections and Technical Services Publication Committee, Library Materials Price Index Editorial Board, comps., "Prices of U.S. and Foreign Published Materials," *Library and Book Trade Almanac 2012*, 57th ed. (New York: Bowker, 2012), 513.

16. "Special Report: Public Library Funding and Technology Access Study 2011–2012," *American Libraries*, Digital Supplement (Summer 2012).

17. Lesley Farmer, "Brace Yourself: SLJ's School Library Spending Survey Shows the Hard Times Aren't Over, and Better Advocacy Is Needed," *School Library Journal* (March 1, 2012), www.schoollibraryjournal.com/slj/articles/surveys/893538-351/brace_yourself_sljs_school_library.html.csp.

18. McKenrick, *Digital Squeeze*.

19. Bo-Christer Björk et al., "Open Access to the Scientific Journal Literature: Situation 2009," *PLoS One* 5, no. 6 (2010), www.plosone.org/article/info%3Adoi%2F10.1371%2Fjournal.pone.0011273.

20. Yassine Gargouri et al., "Green and Gold Open Access Percentages and Growth, by Discipline," presented at the *17th International Conference on Science and Technology Indicators (STI), 5–8 September 5–8, 2012, Montreal, Quebec*, http://arxiv.org/abs/1206.3664.

21. Cecilia Botero, Steven Carrico, and Michele R. Tennant, "Using Comparative Online Journal Usage Studies to Assess the Big Deal," *Library Resources and Technical Services* 52, no. 2 (2008): 61–68.

22. Richard Poynder, "The Big Deal: Not Price but Cost," *Information Today* 28, no. 8 (Sept. 2011), www.infotoday.com/it/sep11/The-Big-Deal-Not-Price-But-Cost.shtml.

23. Jim Mouw, quoted in Carol Tenopir, "A Report on Collection Strategies That Resonate with Librarians," *Library Journal* (Apr. 29, 2010), www.libraryjournal.com/article/CA6727455.html.

24. McKenrick, *Digital Squeeze*.

25. Richard Bleiler and Jill Livingston. Evaluating E-resources, SPEC Kit 316 (Washington, DC: Association of Research Libraries, 2010), 12.

26. Primary Research Group, *Survey of Scholarly Journal and Licensing and Acquisition Practice, 2012 Edition* (New York: Primary Research Group, 2012); Primary Research Group, Library Use of EBooks, 2012 ed. (New York: Primary Research Group, 2011).

27. Primary Research Group, *Library Use of E-books.*

28. *Ebook Usage in U.S. Academic Libraries, Third Annual Survey* (New York: Library Journal, 2012).

29. Wisconsin Public Library Consortium, "Wisconsin Libraries Contribute toward $1 Million E-book Buying Pool," www.wplc.info/?s=digital+download+center&x=0&y=0.

30. Texas State Library and Archives Commission, "Costs Avoided by Local Libraries Due to the TexShare Database Program for the 49 Databases Provided for the Year July 1, 2011—June 30, 2012," www.tsl.state.tx.us/texshare/costavoidance.html.

31. David Stern, "Ebooks from Institutional to Consortial Considerations," *Online* 34, no. 3 (2010): 29–35.

CHAPTER 8

THE FUTURE OF E-CONTENT IN LIBRARIES AND A FEW CONCLUDING THOUGHTS

RAPID AND CONSTANT CHANGES in information technologies and the e-content marketplace have made writing this book challenging. Predicting future developments and key areas that librarians should monitor is an even more ambitious undertaking. This chapter aims to focus on trends that have the potential for significant impact on libraries in the next three to five years. Forecasting is always risky and, by necessity, lacks detail. Consequently, this is the briefest chapter in the book. Because of the uncertain nature of any predictions, the outcomes suggested here could be quite different from reality three to five years hence. The chapter concludes with a few essential concepts for librarians to keep in mind as they navigate the murky future of e-content in libraries.

In 1970, Toffler published the seminal *Future Shock,* in which he observed that the future had arrived prematurely.[1] The rate of change has increased so rapidly that even discerning the direction it is taking is difficult. Several forces are shaping the future of e-content in libraries, and they sometimes seem to be going in different directions. The forces at work involve digital media and other technologies, the publishing and content delivery industry, society and the users of libraries, and libraries themselves. Each has some pull in how the future evolves and the strategic directions that libraries choose.[2]

DIGITAL MEDIA AND OTHER TECHNOLOGIES

Mobile computing in the form of smartphones and tablet devices will dominate personal computing. High-quality, full-color displays will be pervasive and e-content will be redesigned to take full advantage. To make the best e-content choices, libraries will need to understand the capabilities of these devices. Platforms and interfaces must be optimized for mobile computing. The ability to access all types of content at all times through a single device will raise user expectations. Users will demand seamless access to e-content and become impatient with multiple steps and click-throughs to locate and retrieve the content they seek. They will expect full integration within content and third-party applications.

No single mobile device will dominate the market, although some current products will disappear from the market. Content creators and suppliers will develop programming that optimizes content for each device. Users expect true portability. Aggregators will move to make their content accessible to all regardless of the device being used.

Options for data storage will increase, becoming faster, more compact, and cheaper. Network connectivity and bandwidth will continue to grow. Users will expect to download any content discovered to their mobile devices and will routinely download large content files. They will expect to maximize options for annotating content and flagging pertinent portions.

Despite the capacity to download large files, users will want the ability to retrieve and download content selectively. Content, not container, becomes more important. Journal articles are already of greater interest than journal issues. People will begin to think about book chapters in the same manner, and content will become increasingly disaggregated. Discoverability at the chapter level will become more important.

Context-aware computing will increase in importance. Context-aware computing uses information about an end user's activities, connections, and preferences to serve up the most appropriate and customized content, product, or service. In libraries, this might take the form of recommending and providing links to additional content based on current and past search and retrieval activity.

Advances in mobile payment technology will create an environment in which users routinely pay for all types of services and products via a mobile device. Users may find locating e-content and paying providers directly easier and faster than navigating through the complexities of access and delivery found on library websites.

DRM technology will change, and some authors and publishers will make greater use of alternatives, such as digital watermarks, to discourage file sharing. For example, J. K. Rowling's Harry Potter e-books now are sold with watermarks instead of DRM. Publishers and distributors will make their books readable on more than one device, paralleling the move that Apple made when it began selling DRM-free tracks that could be played on various devices (not just iPods) and when Amazon.com began selling DRM-free music.

Streaming media will overtake CDs and DVDs as the preferred medium. Libraries of all types will increase their provision of streaming audio and video.

PUBLISHING AND CONTENT DISTRIBUTION INDUSTRY

Prices for e-content will continue to increase faster than the Consumer Price Index. Book publishers will focus on e-books as the more important segment of their business. More publishers will sell e-books to libraries. Publishers will issue e-books and print versions of the same title simultaneously, eliminating embargo periods. Libraries will be able to move to an e-preferred policy for books without delaying access to current publications. More e-book aggregators and publishers will distribute their books through standard book vendors. This move will permit libraries to expand approval plan profiles and better control duplication of titles and formats.

Business models will evolve and stabilize. E-book publishers will more frequently offer libraries enduring rights to titles, including the right to transfer them to other delivery platforms. E-book publishers will relax their limitations to a single user, although this will come with a higher price, as it does with e-journals. E-book publishers and distributors will offer rent-to-own more widely as an option. In this model, the library pays for each loan and has purchase rights after a specified number of loans, with the total loan payments going toward the purchase price. E-book publishers and distributors who directly serve the public will significantly decrease e-book prices, similar to the trend occurring in the music industry. People may respond by bypassing the library totally, preferring to purchase rather than hassle with borrowing e-books from libraries. E-journal publishers will move away from customized pricing for each library customer because of the time and effort required to reach agreement. Data will show that the costs of managing customized pricing outweigh the benefits for publishers. License restrictions on ILL of e-content will be relaxed. Libraries will spend significantly less time negotiating contracts.

One trend that will continue and not stabilize is the frequency of buyouts, mergers, and sales. Large publishers will purchase smaller publishers. Commercial journal publishers will take over society publications. Although this has the potential to reduce the number of access and delivery platforms and simplify discovery, the growth of large publishers into even larger entities with more extensive title lists will reduce options for libraries.

Aggregators and publishers will move away from requiring library users to search within their proprietary platforms. One approach will be application programming interfaces (APIs) that allow vendors to integrate aggregators and publisher catalogs with vendor applications and platforms. This change will enhance the ability of users to search and browse a single comprehensive catalog of all the library's offerings. Search and retrieval will become less fragmented and cumbersome. Full integration will offer the ability to place holds, check out items, and view availability within the individual library's catalog or discovery layer.

Content suppliers will continue to improve and standardize use statistics. Analytics, the discovery and communication of meaningful patterns in data, will increase in importance to both content providers and libraries. Attention will shift from simply analyzing historical data to explain what happened to analyzing historical and real-time data proactively to simulate and predict future activity.

One aspect of the present content environment that may not change and will likely continue to trouble content users is the balkanization of applications. As readers purchase specific devices and invest in content for those devices, they are less willing to move to another option. If they do, the collections they have assembled become fractured across disparate and outdated systems, making searching and use of these resources more difficult. Library users who legitimately download articles and other content through their libraries face challenges in integrating all this content in a way that is meaningful and useful.

SOCIETY AND LIBRARY USERS

Many demographic trends in the United States have been documented. These include increases in ethnic diversity, an aging population, declining birthrates, a growing portion of Americans living in income-segregated neighborhoods, and a decline in marriage paired with new forms of family units.[3] Although these trends can affect the types of services libraries provide, digital differences in user communities will have the greatest impact on the types of collections libraries develop and how they provide access. The term *digital divide* was introduced in the 1990s to describe the inequalities between demographic and geographic groups in terms of access to, use of, or knowledge of information and communication technologies.[4] At that time, people with lower incomes, those living in rural areas and city centers, and those in racial groups other than white non-Hispanic were less likely to have computers and the ability to connect to the Internet. Libraries served an important role in providing access to computers and the Internet. Remote access to library e-content was a lesser concern.

The future of connectivity will be quite different. Data already show that 63 percent of U.S. adults go online using laptops or cell phones.[5] This percentage varies little by ethnicity. Although higher household income is linked to higher use, 50 percent of households with an income of less than $30,000 a year go online using a laptop or cell phone. As of early 2012, 88 percent of American adults had a cell phone, and this will reach close to 100 percent penetration within three years.[6] Some 46 percent of American adults had a smartphone in February 2012, and this will increase significantly with people increasingly choosing these devices. The Pew Research Center reported, "Groups that have traditionally been on the other side of the digital divide in basic internet access are using wireless connections to go online. Among smart phone owners, young adults, minorities, those with no college experience, and those with lower household income levels are more likely than other groups to say that their phone is their main source of internet access."[7] Libraries must be aware of this trend as they select e-content and choose how to provide discovery and access.[8] Compatibility with mobile devices is essential along with using mobile strategies to reach user communities.

LIBRARIES

Libraries will continue to cope with insufficient funding while struggling to deliver the resources and services users want. The digital squeeze will persist.[9] Libraries will seek supplemental funding sources and look to granting agencies and foundations. They may pass some costs on to their users.

Delivering licensed e-content will continue to be libraries' top priority, continuing the trend reported by OCLC in 2012.[10] Most academic and community college library staff consider delivering licensed e-collections and e-books to be their top priority, and most public library staff focus on e-books as their top initiative. More than 85 percent of academic library expenditures and 60 percent of public library expenditures will be for e-content by 2015. Libraries that have been slow to reconfigure their materials budgets and realign workflow will be forced to do so.

Libraries will optimize their websites for mobile devices because they are the primary Internet access points for a growing number of users. As ownership of mobile devices continues to increase, library patrons will expect greater access to e-books. *Library Journal* reported in July 2012 that 28 percent of library patrons want to download e-books from their local libraries; this percentage will increase rapidly.[11]

Research libraries will continue to follow and support open-access offerings, but the current slow rate of growth in open access will preclude depending on it as a reliable alternative to purchased content. Libraries will continue to rely on subscriptions, pay-per-view, and ILL for most of the scholarly articles their users need.

Big Deals will be dropped by more libraries, which cannot sustain these large packages in the face of modest budget increases or flat or reduced budgets. Libraries will retain the most heavily used journal subscriptions and rely on other delivery options for content from lesser-used titles. Usage data and cost-benefit analysis will become essential for making informed decisions about what to retain and what to cancel.

More libraries will rely on pay-per-view for article delivery, integrated into catalogs and discovery layers in such a way that users will be unaware of whether the library has a subscription or is purchasing individual articles. Options to pay by the chapter will increase as the ability to locate desired content at the chapter level increases. The discovery and delivery experience will be seamless from the user's perspective.

Patron-driven acquisitions will become the primary approach to collection building in academic libraries. Libraries will move away from purchasing large packages of e-books from publishers and aggregators, depending on users to select individual titles that will be used now instead of sometime in the future. Rent-to-own will become a popular option as libraries determine that paying for two or three rentals is cheaper than purchasing. Each library will decide the number of rentals that will trigger a purchase, depending on its user community.

Libraries will add "buy it" links for e-books to their catalogs and discovery layers. Research has shown that library users buy more books.[12] Adding this link, which is consistent with libraries' goals to connect users to resources, may facilitate discounts with publishers.

Increased ease of remote access will mean that patrons have less reason to visit the physical library to access the materials they seek. Libraries will continue to rethink and repurpose how they use their space.

Patron privacy will become an increasing concern for libraries. As more patrons use the Internet to access library services and collections, commercial entities can add information about personal library usage to the records of these individuals' activities, interests, preferences, and location they compile.[13] These data—drawn from searches made, web pages visited, content viewed, interactions on social networking sites, e-mail content, and products and services purchased—are used to deliver targeted advertisements. Many Internet users may be comfortable with more targeted ads and unconcerned about the data collected to make this possible. When, however, this technique mines library use data (as Amazon.com did with Overdrive Kindle use data), patron privacy, a library value, is breached.[14]

Web-scale management and discovery, which provide a single unified solution that streamlines routine tasks, including acquisitions, re-resource management, cataloging, and circulation, will increase in libraries. Their success in providing a single, unified, comprehensive index of traditional library catalog records and article-level content almost instantaneously will simplify user discovery and access, improve success, and increase satisfaction.

CONCLUDING THOUGHTS

How are librarians to plan for a future that feels like it is arriving prematurely? With so many aspects of digital media and technology, publishing and the content industry, society, and libraries themselves in transition, is anything constant? The answer is a resounding yes. The importance of libraries to communities of users persists, and the core values that guide librarians in their work are equally constant. In 2010, Kniffel assembled a list of twelve ways libraries are good for the country, and this list continues to resonate:[15]

1. Libraries sustain democracy.
2. Libraries break down boundaries.
3. Libraries level the playing field.
4. Libraries value the individual.
5. Libraries nourish creativity.
6. Libraries open young minds.
7. Libraries return high dividends.
8. Libraries build communities.
9. Libraries support families.
10. Libraries build technology skills.
11. Libraries offer sanctuary.
12. Libraries preserve the past.

Librarians may find that some of these are more or less relevant to the services and collections their libraries provide, but nearly all are applicable in some way. Kniffel has aptly summarized the continuing importance of libraries to their communities. This will not change.

The American Library Association has codified the core values that continue to guide librarians, library staff, and other professionals in information-providing services in a code of ethics, first adopted in 1939 and since amended:[16]

1. We provide the highest level of service to all library users through appropriate and usefully organized resources; equitable service policies; equitable access; and accurate, unbiased, and courteous responses to all requests.
2. We uphold the principles of intellectual freedom and resist all efforts to censor library resources.
3. We protect each library user's right to privacy and confidentiality with respect to information sought or received and resources consulted, borrowed, acquired or transmitted.
4. We respect intellectual property rights and advocate balance between the interests of information users and rights holders.
5. We treat co-workers and other colleagues with respect, fairness, and good faith, and advocate conditions of employment that safeguard the rights and welfare of all employees of our institutions.
6. We do not advance private interests at the expense of library users, colleagues, or our employing institutions.
7. We distinguish between our personal convictions and professional duties and do not allow our personal beliefs to interfere with fair representation of the aims of our institutions or the provision of access to their information resources.
8. We strive for excellence in the profession by maintaining and enhancing our own knowledge and skills, by encouraging the professional development of co-workers, and by fostering the aspirations of potential members of the profession.

To this can be added a few guiding principles:

- Librarians develop collections and services that support the library's mission and that of its parent organization.

- Librarians exercise good stewardship in managing the library's financial and staffing resources.
- Librarians make data-driven decisions.
- Librarians implement efficiencies that improve operations and services without compromising the quality of those operations and services.
- Librarians employ fair, ethical, and legal practices in dealings with content suppliers, agents, vendors, and their representatives.

Keeping these unchanging attributes, core values, and guiding principles in mind will assist libraries and librarians as they navigate the rapidly changing environment in which they operate. Tradeoffs likely will be necessary, but effective choices can be made.

Notes

1. Alvin Toffler, *Future Shock* (New York: Random House, 1970).
2. Roger E. Levien, *Confronting the Future: Strategic Visions for the 21st Century Public Library*, Policy Brief 4 (Chicago, ALA Office for Information Technology Policy, 2011), www.ala.org/ala/aboutala/offices/oitp/publications/policybriefs/confronting_the_futu.pdf.
3. Mark Mather, Kelvin Pollard, and Linda A. Jacobsen, *First Results from the 2010 Census* (Washington, DC: Population Reference Bureau, 2011), http://prb.org/pdf11/reports-on-america-2010-census.pdf; Richard Fry and Paul Taylor, *The Rise of Residential Segregation by Income* (Washington, DC: Pew Research Center, 2012), www.pewsocialtrends.org/2012/08/01/the-rise-of-residential-segregation-by-income; Pew Research Center, *The Decline of Marriages and Rise of New Families* (Washington, DC: Pew Research Center, 2010), www.pewsocialtrends.org/files/2010/11/pew-social-trends-2010-families.pdf.
4. U.S. Department of Commerce, National Telecommunications and Information Administration, *Falling through the Net: A Survey of the "Have Nots" in Rural and Urban America*, www.ntia.doc.gov/ntiahome/fallingthru.html.
5. Kathryn Zickuhr and Aaron Smith, *Digital Differences* (Washington, DC: Pew Research Center, 2012), http://pewinternet.org/~/media//Files/Reports/2012/PIP_Digital_differences_041312.pdf.
6. Joanna Brenner, "Pew Internet: Mobile" (July 3, 2012), http://pewinternet.org/Commentary/2012/February/Pew-Internet-Mobile.aspx.
7. Zickuhr and Smith, *Digital Differences*, 2.
8. Timothy Vollmer, *There's an App for That: Libraries and Mobile Technology: An Introduction to Public Policy Considerations*, Policy Brief 3 (Chicago: ALA Office for Information Technology Policy, 2010), www.ala.org/offices/files/oitp/publications/policybriefs/mobiledevices.pdf.
9. Joseph McKenrick, *The Digital Squeeze: Libraries at the Crossroads: The Library Resource Guide Benchmark Study on 2012 Library Spending Plans* (Providence RI: Unisphere Research, 2012), www.libraryresource.com/Downloads/Download.ashx?IssueID=3213.

10. OCLC, "U.S. Academic Libraries: A Snapshot of Priorities and Perspectives" (2012), www
    .oclc.org/reports/us-academic-libraries/default.htm; OCLC, "U.S. Community College
    Libraries: A Snapshot of Priorities and Perspectives" (2012), www.oclc.org/reports/us-col-
    lege-libraries/default.htm; OCLC, "U.S. Public Libraries: A Snapshot of Priorities and Per-
    spectives" (2012), www.oclc.org/reports/us-public-libraries/default.htm.

11. "Media Consumption and Library Use," *Library Journal Patron Profiles* 1, no. 4 (July 2012).

12. Steve Paxhia and John Parsons, comps., "Library Patrons and Ebook Usage Analysis," *Library
    Journal Patron Profiles* 1, no. 1 (Oct. 2011).

13. Privacy Rights Clearing House, "Fact Sheet 18: Online Privacy: Using the Internet Safely"
    (rev. July 2012), www.privacyrights.org/fs/fs18-cyb.htm.

14. Deborah Caldwell-Stone, "A Digital Dilemma: Ebooks and Users' Rights," *American Librar-
    ies* (May 5, 2012), http://americanlibrariesmagazine.org/features/05292012/digital-dilemma
    -ebooks-and-users-rights.

15. Leonard Kniffel, "12 Ways Libraries Are Good for the Country," *American Libraries* (Dec. 21,
    2010), www.americanlibrariesmagazine.org/features/12212010/12-ways-libraries-are-good
    -country.

16. American Library Association, *Intellectual Freedom Manual*, 8th ed., "Code of Ethics of the
    American Library Association," www.ifmanual.org/codeethics.

GLOSSARY

Acceptance. The formal, voluntary act of agreeing to an offer, which leads to creating a legally binding **agreement**.

Access. The ability or right to gain entry to and use an electronic product or service.

Acquisition. The process that involves ordering and receipting (or ensuring access is activated for) library materials.

ADA. *See* **Americans with Disabilities Act**.

Aggregated package. A package of content based on agreements between various publishers and the **aggregator**. The content is not necessarily stable; titles may change as agreements between the aggregator and publishers change.

Aggregator. A third party that combines the full text of journals, articles, or books originally published by multiple publishers and provides online access through a common **interface** or **search engine**.

Aggregator database. The searchable collection of digitized materials produced by an **aggregator**.

Agreement. A legally binding understanding and concurrence between two parties, often in a written **contract.** In the licensing context, this term may be capitalized (i.e., "Agreement"), in which case it refers to the contract (along with any appendices, amendments, or exhibits) that codifies the parties' understanding about access to and use of the digital information resources. *See also* **Contract**.

Amendment. Any modification, revision, or addition to a **contract** or **license agreement**. An amendment may be an addition, deletion, or correction.

Americans with Disabilities Act (ADA). A U.S. federal law enacted in 1990 and amended in 2009 that mandates that no individual may be discriminated against on the basis of disability and that functionally equivalent services must be available to individuals with disabilities.

Application programming interface (API). A specification intended to be used as an **interface** by software components to communicate with each other.

Archive. A repository of information. A dark archive is an archive that is inaccessible to the public, typically used for the preservation of content that is accessible elsewhere.

Archive copy. A copy of a work, in printed or digital format, preserved for future use.

Authentication. A process by which a computer system verifies the identity of a user accessing the system or source of communication.

Authorization. A process to determine if an identified user is authorized to perform a function that the user has requested.

Authorized signature. The signature by a person with authority and power to represent and legally bind a party to a written **agreement.**

Authorized use. The specific product use rights and capabilities authorized under the **terms** of the **license**; may also be referred to as "Permitted use."

Authorized user. A person or entity authorized by the **licensor** to access and use an electronic product or service under the **terms** of the **license**. *See also* **Unauthorized user**.

A–Z list. A listing of a library's electronic **serials, databases,** or **e-book** collections, usually available via the library's website and providing direct links from the entry to the serial.

Backlist. A publisher's list of older but still available books. *See also* **Frontlist**.

Backup copy. A copy of digital information made for recovery purposes.

Bandwidth. The rate at which data is transferred; the size of the connections among computers.

Big Deal. A large bundled package of e-journals from a single publisher, usually offering discounted or special pricing, such as a cap on annual price increases. Big Deals generally require a multiyear agreement and limit cancellations.

Book distributor. *See* **Vendor**.

Born digital. Materials that originate in digital form.

Breach. The breaking of the commitments or failure to adhere to the obligations of a **license** or **contract**.

Browser. *See* **Web browser**.

CLOCKSS (Controlled LOCKSS). A not-for-profit partnership between publishers and research libraries that aims to build a dark **archive** for the preservation of web-based scholarly publications; *see also* **LOCKSS**.

Concurrent use. *See* **Simultaneous use**.

Concurrent users. *See* **Simultaneous users**.

Confidentiality. The ability to keep data in confidence, treated as private, and not for distribution to the general public. Confidentiality typically is codified and enforced through a confidentiality agreement or **nondisclosure** agreement.

Consortium. Group of libraries that agree to work together for a common goal or shared purpose. Some consortia are simply buying clubs, others are a closely integrated network of related libraries.

Content provider. A supplier—generally a publisher, **aggregator**, or full-text host—that offers content for sale or lease to libraries.

Contract. A formal, usually legally binding, **agreement** between two parties; the writing (including any appendices, **amendments**, or exhibits) that details the **terms** and conditions of a formal, legally binding agreement between two or more parties. *See also* **Agreement** and **License**.

Copyright. A federal legal regime that grants for a limited time exclusive rights to authors of original, creative works that are fixed in a tangible medium of expression and provides exceptions to those exclusive rights under certain circumstances. In the United States, the current federal law is the Copyright Act of 1976, which is codified at Title 17 of the United States Code (17 U.S.C. §101, *et seq.*). *See also* **Fair use**.

COUNTER (Counting Online Usage of Networked Electronic Resources). An independent organization that oversees an international set of standards and protocols governing the recording and exchange of online usage statistics, known as the COUNTER Codes of Practice.

Coursepack. Copies of materials that instructors assemble for student use in a specified course.

Customer service representative. The employee of a publisher, **vendor, subscription agent, aggregator,** or other supplier of content and services who is responsible for solving problems and meeting needs on a day-to-day basis. *See also* **Sales representative**.

Damages. Monetary compensation for a legal wrong, such as a **breach** of **contract** or breach of a **confidentiality** agreement.

Database. A large, regularly updated file of digitized information (bibliographic records, abstracts, full-text documents, directory entries, images, statistics, etc.), consisting of records of uniform format organized for ease and speed of search and retrieval and managed with the aid of database management system software.

Demand-driven acquisition. *See* **Patron-driven acquisition**.

Deposit account. A fund managed by a **content provider** into which the library deposits money and against which it draws during the year rather than paying individual invoices as they are issued.

Descriptive metadata. **Metadata** used for the discovery and interpretation of a **digital object**.

Digital archive. A long-term storage area in digital format for backup copies of digital files or for digital files that are no longer in active use or high demand.

Digital object. An entity in which one or more content files and their corresponding **metadata** are united, physically or logically, through the use of a digital wrapper.

Digital rights management (DRM). Access control technologies used by hardware manufacturers, publishers, copyright holders, and individuals to limit the use of digital content and devices. DRM is intended to control access to, track, and limit uses of digital works.

Digitization. The process of creating a digital representation of a picture, drawing, film, audio recording, text, or three-dimensional object.

Discretionary purchase. An individual order for an item or items placed that is outside of any existing approval plan, blanket order, **subscription**, or other **nondiscretionary purchase**. *See also* **Firm order**.

Display. The act of retrieving electronic information for the purpose of viewing on a computer terminal screen or monitor.

Distributor. An agent or company that resells, sublicenses, or otherwise makes a product available from the owner to users.

Documentation. Any materials provided with access to or use of an electronic product; documentation may include installation and user manuals, tutorials, reference guides, and the like.

Domain. On the **Internet**, a group of computers whose host names share a common suffix, the domain name. Some important domains are .com (commercial), .edu (educational), .net (network operations), and .gov (U.S. government). *See also* **Domain name**.

Domain name. Address of an **Internet** site; also, an entity's or computer's unique name on the Internet, which is an alphanumeric substitute for Internet site address coordinates. *See also* **IP address**.

Download. To copy or transfer digital information from a **network** to another electronic storage device or media; the process of saving retrieved information from digital information onto a hard drive, disc, or other electronic storage media.

DRM. *See* **Digital rights management**.

E-book (electronic book). A **digital object** specifically designed to be accessible online and read on either a handheld device or personal computer.

E-book reader. A handheld electronic device designed primarily for the purpose of reading **e-books** and e-periodicals; also called an e-book device or e-reader.

E ink. A proprietary type of electronic paper commonly used in mobile devices such as **e-readers** and, to a lesser extent, mobile phones.

E-journal. An electronic journal; periodical literature that is made available as an individual title via an electronic medium.

Electronic data exchange (EDI). The transmission of data between organizations by electronic means; often used in the library environment to facilitate ordering and invoicing using the ILS.

Electronic paper (e-paper). Display technologies designed to mimic the appearance of ordinary ink on paper and thus the experience of reading a book. Unlike conventional backlit flat panel displays that emit light, electronic paper displays reflect light like ordinary paper.

Electronic Publishing (EPUB). An open standard for **e-book** and web publishing from the International Digital Publishing Forum (www.idpf.org), introduced in 2007 as the successor to the Open eBook format. EPUB defines a means of representing, packaging, and encoding structured and semantically enhanced web content for distribution in a single-file format that is platform-independent. EPUB format allows content to be reformatted and optimized to be viewed on portable devices.

Electronic resources management (ERM) **system**. An automated system that tracks a library's e-content and manages details involved with its acquisition, including **subscription** and licensing, usage, cost, access tracking, and data gathering.

Embargo. A limitation on access to a resource, placed by the publisher on distributors of the publisher's data, usually to prevent the cancellation of individual subscriptions. For example, a publisher's own website provides current issues of their e-publications, but an **aggregator**'s website provides only issues older than one year.

End user. An authorized individual or organization that accesses digital information for their own use. The term typically appears in **licenses** and **contracts** involving computer software, whereas the term **user** more commonly appears in license contracts involving digital database resources.

EPUB. *See* **Electronic Publishing**.

E-reader application. Software that can be put on a device (computer, smartphone, tablet computer, etc.) that allows the user to read **e-books** on that device.

Fair use. A legal doctrine stating that persons other than the owner of a copyright have the right to use the copyrighted materials in a reasonable manner without the owner's consent. The U.S. Copyright Act explicitly identifies four interests that may override the rights of the creator or copyright holder: (1) the purpose and character of the use; including its commercial nature; (2) the nature of the copyrighted work; (3) the proportion that was "taken"; and (4) the economic impact of the "taking." *See also* **Infringement**.

File transfer protocol (FTP). Protocol for exchanging files over the **Internet**. FTP is most commonly used to download a file from a **server** or upload a file to a server using the **Internet.**

Financial exigency. A state of financial crisis; commonly, a judicially accepted condition permitting an educational institution to terminate programs, eliminate staff positions, and curtail other expenditures.

Firm order. An order placed with a publisher or **vendor** for a specific title and number of copies.

First sale doctrine. An exception to copyright that generally allows any person or entity who purchases an authorized, legal copy of a protected item to resell, lend, or give away that item. The first sale doctrine, which the U.S. Copyright Act of 1976 codifies at Section 109(a) (17 U.S.C. §109(a)), is a recognized exception to the copyright owner's exclusive right to distribute protected works under Section 106(3) (17 U.S.C. §106(3)).

Force majeure. A contract clause that protects a party from being held liable for a **breach** of **contract** that was caused by unavoidable events beyond the party's control, such as natural disasters or wars.

Frontlist. A publisher's list of newly published titles. *See also* **Backlist**.

FTP. See **File transfer protocol**.

Fund accounting. A system of accounting that emphasizes accountability rather than profitability, used primarily by nonprofit or government organizations. In fund accounting, a fund is a self-balancing set of accounts, segregated for specific purposes.

Governing law. The specified jurisdictional law that governs the **terms** of the **contract** or **license** should a dispute arise. *See also* **Jurisdiction**.

HathiTrust (www.hathitrust.org). A partnership of research institutions and libraries cooperating to ensure that the scanned cultural record is preserved and accessible.

Host. A computer that functions as the beginning and endpoint of data transfers. An **Internet** host has a unique **IP address** and a unique **domain name** or **host name**.

Host name. The unique name by which a computer is identified to a network.

HTML (Hypertext Markup Language). The main markup or authoring language used to create documents on the web. HTML defines the structure and layout of a web document by using a variety of tags and attributes.

HTTP (Hyptertext Transfer Protocol). Application protocol for distributed, collaborative hypermedia information systems. HTTP defines how messages are formatted and transmitted, and what actions web servers and browsers take in response to various commands.

Hypertext. Text displayed on a computer or other electronic device with references (i.e., hyperlinks) to other text that the reader can immediately access, usually by a mouse click or key press sequence.

ILL. *See* **Interlibrary loan**.

ILS. *See* **Integrated library system**.

Indemnity. One party's obligation to insure, shield, or otherwise defend another party against a third-party's claims that result from performance under, or **breach** of, the **agreement**. Also, a legal exception against **liability** or **penalty** for damage or loss; in a **license**, each party may indemnify the other from claims made by a third party based on use of the product.

Infringement. An unauthorized use of a right protected by copyright, patent, or trademark law; a violation of a contractual right.

Integrated library system (ILS). A collection of integrated functional modules, such as acquisitions, circulation, cataloging, serials, and an online public access catalog.

Intellectual property. Ideas, processes, or works of authorship, such as patents, copyrights, trademarks, and trade secrets, that are protected by law.

Interface. The point or process that serves as an intermediary between two components of a data processing system, for example, the screen display that functions as intermediary between a software program and its human users.

Interlibrary loan (ILL). The practice of lending library materials owned or licensed by a library to another library for use by its users.

International Coalition of Library Consortia (ICOLC) (http://icolc.net). An international, informal, self-organized group of primarily higher-education library consortia that addresses issues of common interest among consortium members.

International Standard Book Number (ISBN). A unique numeric commercial book identifier developed by the International Organization for Standardization. Since 2007, ISBNs have contained thirteen digits. Prior to 2007, ISBNs had ten digits.

International Standard Serial Number (ISSN).The standardized international eight-digit number that uniquely identifies serial publications, including electronic serials, independently of their country of publication, language or alphabet, frequency, medium, and other variables.

Internet. A worldwide system of interconnected networks and computers.

Internet Protocol (IP). The principal communications protocol used to route packets of information across network boundaries.

IP. *See* **Internet Protocol**.

IP address. Address consisting of one, two, or three octets of network numbers that uniquely identify a node on the **Internet**. *See also* **Domain name**.

ISBN. *See* **International Standard Book Number**.

ISSN. *See* **International Standard Serial Number**.

ITHAKA (www.ithaka.org). A not-for-profit organization with a mission to help the academic community use digital technologies to preserve the scholarly record and to advance research and teaching in sustainable ways.

Jobber. *See* **Vendor**.

Journal. A **serial** that disseminates original research and commentary on current developments within a specific subject area, discipline, or field of study. Librarians distinguish between journals and magazines, but publishers and users often use the terms interchangeably; for example, *Ladies Home Journal* is considered a **magazine** by librarians.

Jurisdiction. A court's authority to hear arguments, apply law, or decide a legal case or dispute. *See also* **Venue**.

Knowledge base. A centralized repository for information; in library information technology, a machine-readable resource for the dissemination of information about content a library owns or has the rights to access. An **OpenURL link resolver** depends on the completeness and quality of data in the knowledge base to determine if an item (article, book, etc.) is available electronically and what the appropriate copy for a user is.

Lease. A **contract** conveying temporary use rights for a specified period in exchange for rent or other compensation.

Leased content. Content for which the library must pay an annual **subscription** fee or access is lost.

Liability. Legal responsibility for an act or a failure to act.

License. The portion of a **contract** that defines explicitly the rights of the **licensee** to use the product or service provided. A license to use digital information gives a licensee permission to access and use the information under the **terms** and conditions described in the **agreement** between the **licensor** and the **licensee**.

License agreement. A written document, normally in **contract** form, that defines explicitly the **rights** that the **licensor** is granting to the **licensee**, subject to certain conditions and obligations and in exchange for compensation (usually a negotiated fee).

Licensee. The person or entity that receives permission under a **license** to access or use digital information. The licensee, such as a library or educational or research organization, generally pays the **licensor** a fee for permission to use digital information.

Licensor. The party to the **license** that grants the licensed access and use rights. The licensor owns or has permission to distribute digital materials to a **licensee**. If it is representing the interests of copyright owners in a license agreement, the licensor must have the financial means and legal authority to provide the services to which the parties agreed under the license agreement.

Link. A **URL** that references resources integral to the **digital object**.

Link resolver. Application software that uses the **OpenURL** standard to provide context-sensitive linking between a citation in a bibliographic **database** and the electronic full text of the resource cited (article, essay, conference paper, book, etc.) in an **aggregator database** or online from the publisher, taking into account which materials the user is authorized by **subscription** or licensing **agreement** to access.

LOCKSS (Lots of Copies Keep Stuff Safe) (www.LOCKSS.org). An international initiative that provides libraries with digital preservation tools and support to collect and preserve their own copies of authorized e-content.

Magazine. A popular-interest **serial** usually containing articles on a variety of topics, written by various authors in a nonscholarly style. *See also* **Journal**.

Material. Having real importance or great consequences, as in a material **breach** of a contract.

Materials budget. The portion of a library's budget allocated for the acquisition of or access to books, media, **serials**, and other information resources. Some libraries include allocations for postage and service charges associated with acquiring materials and conservation and preservation in the materials budget; others make separate allocations; also may be called "acquisition budget," "access budget," or "collections budget."

Media player. Computer software for playing media files. Media players that can play both audio and video are often called **multimedia** players. Those that focus only on one medium are known as either audio players or video players and often have a user **interface** tailored for the specific medium.

Metadata. Structured data that describe the attributes of a resource, characterize its relationships, and support its discovery, management, and effective use in an electronic environment.

Metasearch tool. One-search access to multiple resources.

Migration. The transfer of digital objects from one hardware or software configuration to another or from one generation of computer technology to a subsequent generation.

Mobile device. A hand-held computing device; may refer to **smartphones, personal digital assistants, tablet computers,** and **e-book readers**.

Monograph. Any nonserial publication, either complete in one volume or intended to be completed in a finite number of successive parts issued at regular or irregular intervals, consisting of a single work or collection of works.

MP3 (MPEG-1 or MPEG-2 Audio Layer III). Patented digital audio encoding format that compresses data by discarding some of it. MP3 is a common audio format for consumer audio storage as well as a de facto standard of digital audio compression for the transfer and playback of music on digital audio players.

Multimedia. A combination of two or more digital media (text, graphics, audio, animation, video, etc.) used in a computer application or data file.

Negotiation. The mutual discussion and arrangement to the **terms** of a **license agreement** until the **licensee** and **licensor** agree on terms and conditions (thereby codifying the agreement in a **contract**).

Network. A hardware- and software-based data communication system consisting of interconnected computers, terminals, workstations, and other electronic resources used to support communication between each element.

Node. A point in a computer **network** where communication lines are connected via a computer or an addressable device attached to a computer network.

Nondisclosure. An **agreement** between parties to protect the **confidentiality** and limit the use of information exchanged.

Nondiscretionary purchase. Any purchase that happens automatically. Examples are **subscriptions**, approval plans, and blanket orders. Nondiscretionary purchases imply a continuing annual commitment against the acquisitions budget.

Nonexclusive rights. Rights that are granted by the **licensor** to multiple **licensees**.

ONIX (Online Information Exchange). A group of standards that supports computer-to-computer communication of **metadata** between the parties involved in creating, licensing, and distributing books (ONIX for Books), serials (ONIX for Serials), and ONIX for Publications Licenses (ONIX-PL). ONIX is used for both physical and digital formats.

Open access. Online resources made openly available to users with no requirements for **authentication** or payment.

Open Archives Initiative–Protocol for Metadata Harvesting (OAI-PMH). A protocol defined by the Open Archives Initiative that provides a method for content providers to make records of their items available for harvesting by services providers.

OpenURL. A framework and format for communicating bibliographic information between applications over the **Internet**. The information provider assigns an OpenURL to an Internet resource instead of a traditional URL. When the user clicks on a link to the resource, the OpenURL is sent to a **link resolver** that resolves the OpenURL to an electronic copy of the resource appropriate for the user (and potentially to a set of services associated with the resource). The OpenURL standard (ANSI/NISO Z39.88–2004, *The OpenURL Framework for Context-Sensitive Services*) specifies the syntax for transporting metadata from information resources (sources) to an institutional link resolver and thence to library services (targets).

Owned content. Content for which the library pays a one-time fee and has access in perpetuity, with a **license** defining the terms of use and archival access.

Owner. The party that legally has or possesses something, such as a copy of the **database** or the **intellectual property** rights.

Package. Group or bundle of titles.

Party. A person or entity that enters into a **contract**.

Patron-driven acquisition. A book purchasing model in which selection decisions are based on input from library patrons. MARC records for books, often matching a profile determined by the library, are loaded into the library's catalog. Once a specific book has been discovered and viewed by a predetermined number of patrons, it is automatically purchased for the collection; also called "demand-driven acquisitions," "patron-initiated purchasing," and "books-on-demand."

Pay-per-view. Online payment in exchange for permission to read an individual document. This is the common means by which readers obtain an individual article or book (or chapter of a book) if they or their organization do not have a **subscription** to or own the resource containing the document. This service is provided by publishers and full-text hosts.

PDA. *See* **Personal digital assistant**.

PDF (Portable Document Format). A file format created by Adobe Systems to be independent of specific hardware and operating systems; a common e-book format.

Penalty. Additional costs assessed due to failure to meet the **terms** of a **license**. A specific cost to be assessed against a party for **breach** of a term of a license.

Periodical. *See* **Serial**.

Permitted use. *See* **Use**.

Permitted user. *See* **User**.

Perpetual access. Contractual rights granted to the buyer or **licensee** that allow access to the electronic product continuing forever.

Perpetual license. The continuing right to access digital information after the termination of a **license agreement**. Also, a **license** with no **termination**.

Personal digital assistant (PDA). A handheld device that combines computing, telephone, and networking features and functions as a personal information manager.

Platform. The fundamental level of a computerized system; may refer to the type of operating system (such as Window or Unix) or the software used to organize and retrieve data.

Portico. A digital preservation service provided by **ITHAKA**, offering reliable, secure access to archived content under specifically defined circumstances. Access is provided when a publication or publishers has experienced a **trigger event**.

Profile. A set of criteria established for an individual user or user group that defines the parameters of a search; profile elements may include terms or phrases, publication dates, specific databases, or Boolean indicators. Also, the criteria that determine titles that will be supplied automatically on a book vendor approval plan or that will appear on periodic notification lists provided by the vendor.

Provider-neutral record. A catalog record representing all online manifestations of a resource made available by multiple online providers.

Proxy server. A **server** (a computer system or an application) that acts as an intermediary for requests from users seeking resources from other servicers. A proxy server replaces the **IP address** of a host on the internal network with its own IP address for all traffic passing through it. Proxy servers are frequently used in the **authentication** remote users of library e-content.

Purchase order. A paper or electronic form a library uses to submit an order to a **vendor**, agent, or publisher.

Registration. The process of entering a unique customer number at the publishers' or other e-content supplier's website and submitting administrative information, such as user name, password, and **IP address** range for the institution, to activate access.

Remedies. The resolutions or corrections available to a party who has been harmed by a **breach**. Remedies can include rights or the cure of a wrong, both at law (in the form of damages) or in equity (in the form of an injunction).

Remote access. The access and use of an electronic product from an off-site (geographically noncontiguous) location.

Request for information (RFI). A document that asks specific questions about the services one or more vendors or agents provide. The purpose of an RFI is to collect written information for comparative purposes. It is often used in combinations with a **request for proposal** and a **request for quotation**.

Request for proposal (RFP). A document listing the requirements and detailed specifications for vendor or agent services along with the steps to be followed for vendors and agents that wish to submit proposals to handle a library's account. RFPs typically are issued for services provided by, for example, monographic vendors, subscription agents, binders, and integrated library systems. Most public agencies use an RFP process in awarding contracts.

Request for quotation (RFQ). A request for pricing based on specification outlined by the purchaser. An RFQ may be part of a **request for information** or specified in a **request for proposal**.

RFI. *See* **Request for information**.

RFP. *See* **Request for Proposal**.

RFQ. *See* **Request for quotation**.

Right of privacy. A generic legal term that covers a variety of personal rights, including the right to be left alone, the right to restrict access to personal information, and the right to control the transfer or distribution of personal information.

Rights. Powers or privileges granted by an **agreement** or law.

Sales representative. An individual charged by a **vendor**, publisher, **aggregator**, or other content or service provider with selling products and services and with resolving general questions or concerns about the products or services already purchased. *See also* **Customer service representative**.

Search. A structured request to a computer system specifying that certain elements be searched within the **database** and the results of the search retrieved for the user.

Search engine. A tool that searches for information on the Web and **FTP** servers. Search results are usually presented in a list of results and are commonly called hits. Examples of popular search engines include Google, Yahoo, Microsoft Bing, and Ask.com.

Security. The procedures in place to prevent **unauthorized users** from accessing a computer or network server; the means used to protect against the unauthorized use of and prevent unauthorized access to digital information.

Serial. A publication issued over a period of time, usually on a regular basis with some sort of numbering used to identify issues, without a foreseeable ending date. Serials may be popular **magazines,** scholarly **journals**, electronic journals, and annual reports. "Serial" is often used interchangeably with the term "periodical" to reflect the periodic nature of its publication.

SERU. *See* **Shared Electronic Resource Understanding**.

Server. A computer that provides services for other terminals and workstations connected to it via a network. A file server provides storage and retrieval capabilities; a printer server provides printing services via a remote printer; a communications server provides access to remote networks and databases.

Service fee. A charge added by a **subscription agent** to the price of a subscription to cover the agent's costs in ordering and managing **subscriptions** for the library.

Shared Electronic Resource Understanding (SERU). A recommended practice of the National Information Standards Organization that allows libraries and publishers to forego a **license agreement** and rely on a mutual understanding of widely accepted practices.

Shibboleth. A standards-based, open-source software that provides web-based single sign-on across or within organizational boundaries. It allows sites to make informed authorization decisions for individual access of protected online resources in a privacy-preserving manner.

Signing authority *Also* **Signature authority**. The authority to bind a party to, approve, or execute a **contract** on that party's behalf. If an individual signs a contract beyond his or her authority, that individual may be held personally liable for enforcing the contract or paying damages on the contract.

Simultaneous use. The limit of access to or use of an electronic product based on the number of simultaneous users.

Simultaneous users. The number of users who may access simultaneously a digital information resource.

Single user model. Only one user may use a title at a time, with the user's access to that title expiring after a specified length of time.

Site. Physical location affiliated with the **licensee** where an electronic product may be accessed and used by an **authorized user**; normally defined by buildings, offices, campuses, or geographic boundaries.

Site license. A **license** that normally allows unlimited use of a product at specified site.

Smartphone. A mobile phone with advanced software, usually providing facilities for connecting to the **Internet** and browsing websites.

Sole source justification. An official statement or confirmation that only one person or company can provide the contractual services or product needed and any attempt to obtain bids would only result in one person or company being available to meet the need.

Standardized Usage Statistics Harvesting Initiative (SUSHI). A National Information Standards Organization recommended practice to be used in creating reports and services related to harvesting electronic resource usage data using a web services framework.

Standing order. An authorization to make regular or periodic shipments of new issues, new editions, or supplementary content for a specified product.

Streaming. Continuous delivery of audiovisual media over telecommunication networks, as opposed to broadcasting (radio and television), at the user's request or at a fixed time, which allows viewing to begin before the entire file has been transmitted. Streaming media is stored as a temporary file and deleted when the application used to view it is closed.

Subject-based packages. Collections of titles focused on a defined subject area.

Subscriber. The party to the **agreement** that is purchasing, leasing, or licensing a product or service; used in the context of an agreement, the subscriber may include all **authorized users**.

Subscription. An **agreement** between a content provider and a subscriber that provides a product or service to the subscriber for a period of time in exchange for a periodic fee.

Subscription agent. A company that specializes in managing subscriptions to content for libraries for a fee. The agent places orders, manages renewals and cancellations, provides consolidated invoicing, and offers other value-added services.

SUSHI. *See* **Standardized Usage Statistics Harvesting Initiative**.

Tablet computer. A mobile computer integrated into a flat touch screen and primarily operated by touching the screen rather than using a physical keyboard; also called a "tablet."

TCP/IP. *See* **Transmission Control Protocol/Internet Protocol**.

Term. The agreed-upon period of time in which a **license** or **contract** is in effect.

Termination. The ending, cancellation, or discontinuance of a **license** or **contract**.

Terms. The individual clauses or sections of a **contract**.

Transmission Control Protocol/Internet Protocol (TCP/IP). Two core communication protocols in the Internet Protocol Suite. TCP enables two computers to establish a virtual connection and exchange streams of data. TCP guarantees delivery of data and also guarantees that packets are delivered in the same order in which they were sent. IP relays network packets of information from the source computer to the destination computer. IP specifies the format of packets and the addressing scheme.

Trial. Limited opportunity for a library to test an e-content product prior to deciding whether to add it.

Trigger event. An occurrence that opens access to a digital archive of commercial content. Typical trigger events are when a publisher ceases operations and titles are no longer available from any other source, when a publisher ceases to publish and offer a title and it is not offered by another publisher or entity, when back issues are removed from a publisher's offering and are not available elsewhere, and upon catastrophic failure by a publisher's delivery platform for a sustained period of time.

Unauthorized user. Any person or entity designated in the **license** who does not have permission to access or otherwise use the digital information that is the subject matter of an **agreement**. Also, any user that the license does not explicitly define as an **authorized user**.

Uniform resource identifier (URI). A standard syntax for locating files using existing Internet protocols, as with a URL.

Upload. To send a file over a **network**.

URL (uniform resource locator). A string of characters that represents the location of a resource on the **Internet** and indicates which program should be invoked to access the resources.

Usability. The effectiveness, efficiency, and satisfaction with which users can achieve tasks, using a particular electronic product.

Use. A licensee's right to operate the **licensor**'s program, software, website, or other electronic environment in order to access the digital information the **licensee** is leasing under an **agreement**. *See also* **Authorized use**.

User. Any person or entity who interacts with licensed digital resources or puts these resources into service. In a **contract**, the term "user," whether in singular or plural, typically is synonymous with **authorized user**. *See also* **Authorized user**, **End user**, **Simultaneous users**, **Unauthorized user**.

Vendor. A supplier or provider of goods and services through which libraries obtain resources instead of dealing directly with a publisher; sometimes called a **distributor**.

Venue. The particular **jurisdiction** where a party brings a legal dispute, which may be where the cause of action arose, where the parties reside, or where the parties conduct business.

Waiver. The voluntary and deliberate relinquishment of rights or claims granted by a **license** or **contract**.

Warranty. An enforceable promise or legally binding written guarantee; typical warranties include quality, performance, or suitability for a specified purpose.

Web browser. A software application for retrieving, presenting, and traversing information resources on the **Internet**. Commonly used web browsers are Microsoft's Internet Explorer, Mozilla's Firefox, Apple's Safari, and Google's Chrome.

XML (Extensible Markup Language). XML is a pared-down version of Standard Generalized Markup Language (SGML), designed especially for web documents. It enables web authors and developers to create their own customized tags to provide enhanced functionality.

Note

This glossary has been compiled from various sources, including these:

CNET: The Computer Network Glossary, www.cnet.com/Resources/Info/Glossary.

Johnson, Peggy. *Fundamentals of Collection Development and Management,* 2nd ed. (Chicago: American Library Association, 2009).

LibLicense: Licensing Digital Content, "Licensing Vocabulary," http://liblicense.crl.edu/resources/licensing-vocabulary.

Reitze, Joan M. "ODLIS: Online Dictionary for Library and Information Science," www.abc-clio.com/ODLIS.

Wikipedia, www.wikipedia.org.

INDEX

You may also be interested in

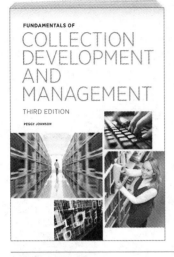

FUNDAMENTALS OF COLLECTION DEVELOPMENT AND MANAGEMENT
Third Edition

PEGGY JOHNSON

Johnson offers a comprehensive tour of this essential discipline and situates the fundamental ideas of collection development and management in historical and theoretical perspective, bringing this modern classic fully up to date.

ISBN: 978-0-8389-1191-4
400 pages / 6" x 9"

CUSTOMER-BASED COLLECTION DEVELOPMENT
An Overview

KARL BRIDGES, EDITOR
ISBN: 978-0-8389-1192-1

BUILDING AND MANAGING E-BOOK COLLECTIONS
A How-To-Do-It Manual for Librarians

EDITED BY RICHARD KAPLAN
ISBN: 978-1-55570-776-7

USER STUDIES FOR DIGITAL LIBRARY DEVELOPMENT

MILENA DOBREVA, ANDY O'DWYER, PIERLUIGI FELICIATI
ISBN: 978-1-85604-765-4

MANAGING ELECTRONIC RESOURCES
A LITA Guide

EDITED BY RYAN O. WEIR
ISBN: 978-1-55570-767-5

CATALOGUE 2.0
The Future of the Library Catalogue

EDITED BY SALLY CHAMBERS
ISBN: 978-1-55570-943-3

RECORDS AND INFORMATION MANAGEMENT

PATRICIA C. FRANKS
ISBN: 978-1-55570-910-5

Order today at alastore.ala.org or 866-746-7252!

ALA Store purchases fund advocacy, awareness, and accreditation programs for library professionals worldwide.